FUNDRAISING FOR SPORT AND RECREATION

William F. Stier, Jr., EdD
State University of New York, Brockport

Human Kinetics Publishers

Library of Congress Cataloging-in-Publication Data

Stier, William F.
  Fundraising for sport and recreation / William F. Stier, Jr.
    p. cm.
  ISBN 0-87322-400-0
  1. Sports--United States--Finance. 2. Recreation--United States-
-Finance. 3. Fund raising--United States--Handbooks, manuals, etc.
4. Nonprofit organizations--United States--Finance--Handbooks,
manuals, etc. I. Title.
GV716.S73 1994
338.4'3796--dc20   93-14556

ISBN: 0-87322-400-0

Photo Credits: Page 15: By Jim Dusen/SUNY College at Brockport; Page 59:
Dancin' Memories; Page 113: Courtesy of Lakeside Foundation, Inc.; Page 155:
Amusements of Rochester.

Acquisitions Editor: Richard D. Frey, PhD; **Developmental Editor**: Julia
Anderson; **Assistant Editors**: Julie Lancaster, Lisa Sotirelis, and Sally Bayless;
Copyeditor: Julie Anderson; **Proofreader**: Tom Rice; **Production Director**:
Ernie Noa; **Typesetting and Text Layout**: Yvonne Winsor and Tara Welsch;
Text Design: Jody Boles; **Cover Design**: Jack Davis; **Interior Art**: Tim
Offenstein; **Printer**: Versa Press, Inc.

Printed in the United States of America   10 9 8 7 6 5 4 3 2 1

Human Kinetics Publishers
Box 5076, Champaign, IL 61825-5076
1-800-747-4457

Canada: Human Kinetics Publishers, Box 24040, Windsor, ON N8Y 4Y9
1-800-465-7301 (in Canada only)

Europe: Human Kinetics Publishers (Europe) Ltd., P.O. Box IW14,
Leeds LS16 6TR, England
0532-781708

Australia: Human Kinetics Publishers, P.O. Box 80, Kingswood 5062,
South Australia
618-374-0433

New Zealand: Human Kinetics Publishers, P.O. Box 105-231, Auckland 1
(09) 309-2259

To my wife, Veronica, and our five children—Mark, Missy, Michael, Patrick, and Will III—for their loving encouragement and unselfish support.

Contents

Preface

This is a practical, user-friendly book that provides a variety of proven methods of generating money and enthusiasm for sport, recreation, and leisure programs. The ideas and methods suggested within this book are based upon proven, successful fundraising concepts. The fundamental fundraising guidelines that are clearly illustrated in this primer should be a great boon to individuals facing the formidable task of raising money for sport or recreation organizations.

With less and less money available for organizations through the regular budgetary process, there is an ever-increasing need for outside promotional and fundraising activities. Today, individuals in almost every sport and recreation organization and educational institution are finding themselves financially pinched. This book was written to help those who face the challenge of generating financial support for worthwhile sport and recreational activities.

This includes recreation leaders and administrators; individuals responsible for fundraising for various nonprofit, social organizations such as the Boy Scouts, Girl Scouts, YMCA/YWCAs, and Boys Clubs of America; coaches and athletic administrators of youth sport teams such as Little League baseball, soccer teams, youth hockey organizations, and midget football squads; booster club members for youth sport and for junior and senior high sports; and, of course, coaches and athletic administrators at junior and senior high schools, junior colleges, and four-year colleges and universities. In fact, many of these individuals assisted me as I wrote this book by sharing their ideas, suggestions, and critiques.

This book has been written for sport and recreation practitioners out on the firing line who are seeking fundraising ideas to use in their organizations. In these pages are practical ideas on how to plan, conduct, and evaluate a variety of successful fundraising projects. These are projects that can generate money and enhance program image.

Many of these fundraisers can simply be lifted from this book and duplicated in your community with very little change. Other fundraising projects in this book might require substantial alterations and adaptations in order to be successfully implemented for your organization. Thus, this book can be likened to a cookbook; the various fundraising projects are recipes which, if followed even with some changes, will enable you to plan and implement highly successful fundraising events to suit your own tastes.

These fundraising projects are also a starting point from which you can devise your own unique fundraising projects to meet your particular needs. The material in this book is organized so that you will learn what you must do to plan, implement, and bring to closure a profitable, effective, and efficient fundraising event. This book will help you to better understand the processes and tasks involved in generating money in light of restrictions or limitations under which you might be working as well as the resources available to you.

This book is divided into several sections. The first explains how to use the book and provides some basic fundraising theories as well as suggestions and guidelines for holding successful fundraising events. This is followed by a "Fundraiser Finder," which serves as an index of the 70 fundraisers presented in this book. The fundraisers themselves are divided into four sections based on their potential net profit, the amount that you can reasonably expect to raise.

Material about the fundraising events includes all of the information you need to plan, implement, and conclude the activity. This information includes an explanation and a detailed description of the project; the potential income and other benefits relative to the effort expended; suggestions about when to plan and hold the event; time requirements to plan and implement the project; the degree of complexity of the activity; the resources needed in terms of facilities, seed money, equipment, and supplies; suggested publicity and related promotional activities; staffing and personnel requirements; information about any necessary permits or licenses; tips for managing potential financial and legal risks; and specific hints for the success of the project.

The information about specific events and the general fundraising principles in the "How to Use This Book" section enable you to accomplish two objectives. First, you can develop a basic understanding of the components necessary for making any fundraising project a success—the fundamentals of fundraising for sport and recreation. Second, you will learn how to apply this basic knowledge, coupled with your own ideas and your understanding of your own needs, to plan and implement an actual fundraising activity. It is this pragmatic presentation of fundraising theory that makes this book of unique value to organizers of fundraising events in the world of sport and recreation.

How to Use This Book

Sport and recreation have never been more popular in the United States than today. However, accompanying this increase in participation has been an increase in the cost of providing and conducting meaningful sport and recreational activities. Recreation leaders, coaches, and sport administrators are painfully aware of the financial crunch facing almost all organizations that provide sport and recreation programs. This is true whether such activities are provided within the structure of an educational setting, a youth sport organization, a recreation department, or some other nonprofit entity.

The financial needs of sport and recreation programs must be met if these programs are to continue to exist and to meet the needs of the individuals they serve. Without adequate funding sport and recreation programs, whatever their intrinsic value, are probably doomed to failure. Thus, securing financial support is rapidly being recognized as one of the prime responsibilities (and challenges) facing recreation leaders, sport administrators, and athletic coaches.

In fact, the ability to secure adequate funding is considered an essential, indispensable skill in the operation of any sport or recreation program. The sport leader who is a competent fundraiser is viewed as a highly valuable asset to any organization. As a result, fundraising has become a fact of life for those of us in sport, recreation, and leisure programs.

A successful fundraising event is one that satisfies four major objectives. First, it is financially successful; it makes money that you can use to support your organization's many worthwhile activities. Second, the event generates enthusiasm for the fundraising project itself. Third, the event helps foster and reinforce a positive image of your organization and its supporters through the exposure, publicity, and public relations associated with the activity itself. Fourth, the event generates genuine support for the overall efforts and goals of the sponsoring organization.

Those in charge of fundraising will find that their individual situations are usually somewhat different, sometimes radically different, from the situations in which others must operate. Sometimes specific resources (such as facilities, personnel, equipment, supplies, money, and image) are not available or are inadequate for a particular project. Frequently there are limitations (related to finances, programs, public relations, image, reputation, competition, and location) that will restrict your activities.

Thus, you must look at each of the fundraising projects with a critical eye to see if the suggestions can indeed help simplify or improve some aspect of the fundraising process, if not the total project itself. You must determine what will work and what will not work in your own community in light of the resources available and the limitations that exist.

I suggest that you read through all of the fundraising projects included in this book to develop a clearer understanding of the similarities and differences between the various methods of fundraising. Many projects contain information and suggestions that are applicable to other fundraising efforts.

Certainly you should examine carefully all of the projects that use similar fundraising concepts. For example, if you are thinking of holding an auction at the local level, it will be of great help to read all of the fundraising projects in this book that use the auction method. Similarly, there are several fundraising efforts that use the sales concept, and there are several activities that involve food or a concession operation. Reading all of the projects that are based upon the same concept will enhance your understanding and competency level in terms of creating, developing, and implementing a successful fundraising program.

How This Book Is Organized

Following this introduction is a "Fundraiser Finder," which will help you quickly decide which fundraiser will be suitable for your organization. In the "Fundraiser Finder" each of the fundraising projects is listed and is assigned an identifying number. To the right of each fundraiser are listed the potential dollar profit, the complexity of the event, the number of people who should be involved in planning and implementing the project, the amount of money needed to finance the fundraiser, and the page number in the book where the event is described in detail.

The various fundraising projects presented in the book are provided in identical formats for ease of comparison and understanding. Details concerning each project are shared in light of the following factors.

Potential Net Income

An estimated net profit is provided for each fundraising project. Of course, profit can vary from event to event and from community to community, so the figures provided are only estimates.

Complexity/Degree of Difficulty

Complexity is indicated by the words *low*, *moderate*, and *high*. These words indicate the amount of work and time generally involved in planning and implementing the project. Of course, the complexity of any event depends upon the sponsoring organization's resources, restrictions, and community climate. What might be difficult for one group might not be as difficult for another.

Description

This section explains what the project is all about and discusses details of the event that must be addressed if it is to be successful. Naturally, you need to account for circumstances within your organization and in your community when planning, organizing, and implementing any fundraiser.

Scheduling

This information includes techniques and strategies for successful event scheduling.

Resources

This general heading is broken down into the following categories, which provide a detailed glimpse into the resources you will need.

Facilities. This describes what facilities, if any, are needed and the type of facilities that will best suit the fundraising event. Also, suggestions are made as to whether you can secure the use of the facilities at reduced or no cost.

Equipment and Supplies. Most fundraising efforts involve some type of equipment and supplies. Those items deemed necessary are listed, and suggestions are included on how you can obtain and best utilize such items, preferably at reduced or no cost.

Publicity and Promotion. Suggestions regarding the use of publicity and promotional tactics are presented for each fundraising project. The timing of such promotional efforts is discussed, when appropriate.

Time. Here information is presented concerning time requirements, both for the actual event as well as for the planning and implementation stages.

Expenditures. In many instances, it costs money to make money. This information will give you an idea of how much money you might have to spend, and for what, in order to conduct the fundraiser. Ideas on how to save money are also shared. *Generally, you should avoid spending money whenever possible.* Rather, you should always attempt to obtain tools, assets, and resources for free or at reduced cost. If you need poster boards, ask for donations. If signs need to be painted, find someone who will donate time and expertise. Of course money will have to be spent in many projects. When fundraising projects involve the selling of items, organizers frequently will need to purchase (at reduced cost) the items that are to be sold; this is part of the cost of sales. There is no magic formula or fixed percentage that you can use as a benchmark in determining how much money should be spent to raise a specific dollar amount. Naturally, the less money spent the better. But the amount will depend upon your specific situation.

Personnel (Staff/Volunteers). Every fundraising effort depends upon personnel, both paid staff of the sponsoring organization as well as volunteers or boosters. Under this category are suggestions regarding the approximate number of people who should be involved with the event and their principle responsibilities and tasks.

Risk Management

This category deals with legal risks, such as liability concerns and insurance matters, as well as financial risks, which could prove disastrous for the would-be fundraiser if not accounted for. Risk management involves examining worst-case scenarios and then making plans to avoid or minimize, as much as possible, such negative consequences.

Permits/Licenses

This category tells you how to secure any permits, licenses, or permissions you may need in order to carry out the project.

Hints

This category is reserved for specific suggestions to help you plan, execute, and evaluate the fundraising event. Additionally, insight into alternative ways to conduct the specific event is provided. You should take these hints with a grain of salt, so to speak, in light of individual resources and limitations in your community and within the sponsoring group itself.

Gambling and Games of Chance

Special note should be taken of fundraising efforts that involve gambling or games of chance. Many states and communities have laws or ordinances either prohibiting or restricting games of chance and gambling activities.

Thus, activities that generate money via gambling might very well be strictly regulated by law or ordinance. Conducting games of chance or gambling projects without securing the appropriate permits or licenses, when such are required, can result in serious legal and punitive actions against you as well as against the sponsoring organization. Conscientious fundraisers make sure they meet all legal obligations. *Never* take a chance by assuming law enforcement agencies may overlook the lack of a permit.

Those fundraising organizers who abide by the philosophy of "forgiveness is easier to obtain than permission" need to be aware of the possible negative consequences of illegally conducting gambling activities. These consequences can be severe in terms of not only legal penalties but also negative publicity and tarnished image. The best course is to check with your organization's legal counsel before attempting to organize a fundraising project based on gambling or games of chance.

In the state of New York, for example, organizations wishing to conduct such games must secure advance permission from both the New York State Racing and Wagering Board and from the local municipality (through the town clerk) where the event will take place. New York state provides two different kinds of permits, one for bingo and one for games of chance. The cost of conducting a bingo game is $18.75 per event whereas games of chance cost $25 per day. An additional requirement is that a financial statement must be submitted to the state within a specified number of days following the event.

Alcoholic Beverages

In order to serve alcoholic beverages at a fundraising event, you must first secure the necessary state and/or local liquor licenses or permits. The permits required vary among locales. Some jurisdictions require one specific permit for hard liquor (scotch, whiskey, vodka, gin, etc.) and another for light spirits (beer, wine, and champagne). Other areas require a specific license if alcohol will be served with food and not purchased separately. Still another permit may be issued when a cash bar will be provided, and another when alcohol will be dispensed on a free basis. You must secure the appropriate permits for your individual community. Of course, the sponsoring organization may have other restrictions or prohibitions against serving alcohol, so check ahead of time to see what is permitted and what is prohibited.

Organizers of a fundraising event where alcoholic beverages are served must also be alert to a situation in which a patron is becoming intoxicated. The negative consequences are significant not only for the patron but also for the sponsoring organization and the person who served the alcohol. Sponsors and planners of an event where a person consumes an excessive amount of alcohol are increasingly being held responsible for that person's actions. No sport or recreation group wants to be involved in a DWI scandal, so those responsible for planning and implementing the fundraising project must take assertive action to prevent both underage drinking and overindulgence by those of legal age.

- Post signs indicating that patrons will be asked for appropriate identification, and then carefully scrutinize the IDs.
- Make arrangements with a local cab company to drive home patrons who have overindulged in drink, or provide designated drivers from among the volunteers of the sponsoring group.
- Encourage people attending the event to team up with friends who are willing to be designated drivers.

These plans will help prevent negative consequences of excessive alcohol consumption and driving under the influence and will enhance the public's image of the sponsoring organization as sensible, caring, and proactive.

Sales

Many fundraising projects involve selling, and many direct sales efforts, especially door-to-door sales, involve youngsters and volunteers. Whenever young people are expected to sell door-to-door, they need to first receive appropriate safety instruction and sales training. Common safety rules instruct children to travel in pairs, be accompanied by an adult or older sibling, sell only within their own neighborhood unless accompanied by an adult, obey all traffic laws, and not venture out after dusk.

Teaching students and volunteers how to sell successfully means teaching how to

- identify potential customers,
- approach them,
- explain the product,
- emphasize the benefits to the purchaser,
- explain the nature of the nonprofit sponsoring organization,
- clarify how the money will benefit young people and sport or recreation programs,
- handle objections,
- thank the prospect whether or not a purchase was made,
- and maintain accurate records.

Overaggressive or hard-sell tactics should be strongly discouraged.

Sales Tax

Laws vary regarding the collection of sales tax for fundraising activities by nonprofit organizations. The question of whether it is necessary to collect sales tax frequently arises when the sponsoring organization sells tickets, merchandise, or concession items. The county tax collector or a representative of the state department of revenue will be able to answer many questions in this regard. Or, consult a competent attorney or accountant to obtain an expert opinion about this complicated area.

Permits, Licenses, and Permission

Some fundraising activities involve door-to-door sales of items such as tickets, candy, chances, or almost anything, both tangible and intangible. More and more communities are passing ordinances that prohibit, restrict, or regulate door-to-door sales.

Some communities have implemented ordinances that restrict the activities of so-called transient retail merchants. A transient retail business is frequently defined as a business conducted for less than 6 months; it can be located in the street, on the sidewalk, in front of a building, or within a building, motor vehicle, or tent. Typically, the transient retail merchant ordinance is aimed at restricting or regulating flower vendors, furniture salespersons, car washers, and art merchants who display their merchandise and services at street intersections or in parking lots.

Licensing fee exemptions commonly exist for charitable organizations, groups from area school districts or colleges, recreation departments, city-sponsored organizations, and nationally recognized service organizations or clubs. However, not all communities provide such blanket exemptions. Thus, you should check with the local municipal office that issues permits or licenses (most likely the town clerk) to see what you must do before initiating a fundraising effort that might fall under the local hawking, peddling, and soliciting ordinance.

When concession or food operations are involved in a fundraising project it is essential that you follow all health department regulations for food storage, preparation, and sale and that you secure all appropriate permits and licenses that regulate food and concession operations. Typically, such permits may be secured from the municipal offices or the office of the town clerk.

Of course, securing permission and various permits and licenses is only half the battle. The other half is adequately informing the paid staff and volunteers about what the permits, licenses, and permissions require and allow. In particular, the licenses and permits that regulate food and door-to-door sales have many restrictions that must be strictly adhered to. Organizers of an event have the responsibility to see that the staff, paid and volunteer, fully understand and abide by the constraints of the licenses.

Record Keeping

Successful fundraising is not possible without accurate and timely record keeping. Everyone involved must keep some kind of records: the organizers and planners of the fundraising projects, the young people and other volunteers, and even the booster clubs or athletic support groups. Some of the documentation that is often kept includes records of prospects, past donors, customers, alumni, inventory, vendors, budgets, income, expenses, pledges, items purchased for later sale, insurance, taxes, permits and licenses, minutes or summaries of meetings, copies of letters received and sent, and evaluations of past fundraising projects.

One area of concern to all fundraisers is money. Two key words where money is concerned are *accountability* and *security*. Many schools and recreation departments require that all income from fundraising efforts be deposited in a special activity account. They also require that periodic reports of expenses and income (reconciliations and audits) be made to appropriate parties. Additionally, all checks issued on such accounts usually require at least two (and sometimes three) signatures. Organizers need to pay special attention to financial record keeping; nothing can tarnish the reputation of a fundraising organization more effectively than mistakes or scandals associated with the handling of money.

Combining Fundraising Activities

A strategy that many promoters use to maximize fundraising profits is to combine activities. For example, the addition of a concession stand at an auction site can increase the potential profit for the total experience. Thus, always be on the lookout for ways to increase profitability and enhance exposure by staging two or more activities at the same time and site. Another example is the annual craft show combined with a free car wash. People driving to the craft show might well be enticed to have their vehicles washed for free (see Fundraiser 15), which provides two distinct profit centers for the organizers.

There Is More Than One Way to Do Anything

There is no single way to conduct any specific fundraising project. Fifty different organizations could devise fifty different ways to organize and implement one type of event.

Thus, it is up to you to decide whether to copy exactly the projects outlined in this book or to adapt the ideas and concepts to suit your situation.

Good luck in your search for a suitable fundraising project to fit your needs. After reading this book you will have a sound understanding of each of these projects. Better still, you should possess a better overall concept of the components of the fundraising process itself. And, best of all, you will be able to use ideas and tactics outlined in this book to plan and implement any number of fundraising projects that will net your organization increased enthusiasm for your event, genuine support for your overall efforts and goals, a more positive public image, and additional resources.

Fundraiser Finder

Fundraiser	Number	Net profit	Complexity	Number of people needed	Seed money needed	Page
Annual Fall Bazaar	51	$10,000	High	80-85	$750	148
Annual Garage Sale	13	$2,500	Moderate	22-28	$25	43
Antique and Custom Car and Truck Show	61	$15,000	High	30-45	$750	180
Birthday Cakes for Students	40	$6,000	Moderate	10-15	$250	116
Car Raffle	57	$15,000	Moderate	40-50	$100	168
Car Wash	7	$600	Low	31-42	$25	29
Casino Royale	56	$15,000	High	28-45	$1,000	165
Celebrity Athletic Contest	35	$5,000	Moderate	20-35	$200	104
Celebrity Autograph and Photo Session	33	$5,000	Moderate	10-15	$150	98
Celebrity Sports Dinner	64	$20,000	High	39-61	$750	188
Coaching Clinic of Champions	52	$10,000	High	36-42	$500	151
Coed Fashion Show	23	$3,500	High	30-50	$100	70
Concession Stand	2	$250	Moderate	30-45	$200	18
Consignment Sales	1	$150	Moderate	10-15	$35	16
Country and Western Dance With Lessons	30	$4,000	Moderate	21-31	$500	89
Cow Drop	45	$9,000	Moderate	30	$300	130
Dance Marathon	69	$35,500	High	30	$500	203
Demolition Dividends	67	$27,500	High	42-64	$250	197
Dinner With the Coach/ Administrator	12	$2,500	Low	31-43	$100	41
Donkey Baseball	22	$3,500	Moderate	20-30	$500	67
Event Sponsorship by Business	26	$4,000	Moderate	2-3	$100	78

(continued)

Fundraiser Finder (*continued*)

Fundraiser	Number	Net profit	Complexity	Number of people needed	Seed money needed	Page
50-50 Drawing	46	$10,000	Low	25-30	$100	133
5-Kilometer Race	42	$8,000	Moderate	15-25	$300	121
Flea Market	65	$24,000	High	45-60	$2,000	191
Free Car Wash	15	$3,000	Moderate	31-42	$25	48
Generic Auction	34	$5,000	Moderate	30-50	$150	101
Ghost Marathon	25	$4,000	Low	15-20	$200	76
Golf Tournament	49	$10,000	High	36-52	$250	142
Halloween Haunted House	39	$5,500	High	25-50	$500	114
Hoop-a-Thon	43	$8,500	Moderate	11-14	$50	124
House Tour	29	$4,000	Moderate	30-60	$300	86
Installing Vending Machines	14	$3,000	Low	1	$0	46
Life Insurance Policy Naming Your Organization as the Beneficiary	70	$50,000	High	5-10	$200	206
Marathon Party Night	18	$3,000	Moderate	20-40	$150	55
Marketing Second-Hand Sport Helmets	9	$1,000	Low	5-10	$75	34
Merchandising Campaign	20	$3,500	Moderate	50-125	$0	63
Mile of Art Show	50	$10,000	High	33-50	$500	145
Mums for Sale	17	$3,000	Moderate	37-53	$100	52
Ongoing Bingo Contests	68	$30,000	High	11-17	$300	200
Overnight Youth Sport Summer Camp	44	$8,800	High	20-35	$500	127
Pancake Breakfast	31	$4,000	High	35-40	$250	92
Parking Arrangements for Special Events	10	$1,500	Moderate	40-55	$100	36
Peewee Wrestling Tournament	28	$4,000	Moderate	28-35	$150	83

Fundraiser	Number	Net profit	Complexity	Number of people needed	Seed money needed	Page
Phone-a-Thon	48	$10,000	Moderate	10-45	$150	139
Postevent Miniauction	6	$500	Moderate	20-25	$10	27
Professional Wrestling Exhibition	37	$5,000	Moderate	23-37	$500	108
Progressive Dinner	19	$3,000	High	36-48	$50	60
Pseudo Dinner Invitation	24	$4,000	Low	10-20	$250	73
Publishing a Cookbook	53	$12,000	Moderate	27-35	$200	156
Renting Facility to Outside Groups	3	$250-$500	Low	2-3	$50	21
Selling Advertising Space in a Facility	55	$15,000	Moderate	3-15	$200	162
Selling a Souvenir Sport Publication	54	$13,000	Moderate	45-70	$100	159
Selling Athletic Apparel	38	$5,000	Moderate	10-25	$1,000	111
Selling Bricks for a Memorial Sidewalk/ Patio	58	$15,000	High	31-47	$500	171
Selling Buttons and Pins	5	$500	Low	26-32	$50	25
Selling Coupon Books	62	$15,000	High	37-53	$3,000	183
Selling Holiday Window Decals	21	$3,500	Moderate	50-100	$50	65
Selling Products From National Fundraising Companies	47	$10,000	Moderate	30-300	$0	136
Selling Programs	32	$5,000	Low	16-22	$50	95
Selling Pseudo Deeds	63	$20,000	Moderate	36-53	$200	186
Selling Sport/Activity Posters	11	$2,000	Low	21-32	$50	39

(continued)

Fundraiser Finder (*continued*)

Fundraiser	Number	Net profit	Complexity	Number of people needed	Seed money needed	Page
Sporting Event Buy-Out Nights	16	$3,000	Moderate	10-15	$100	50
Sports Dinner Catered by Athletes and Coaches	60	$15,000	High	70-85	$500	177
Summer Amusement Carnival	59	$15,000	High	28-47	$500	174
Triad Fundraising Evening	66	$25,000	High	42-55	$500	194
Walk-a-Thon	27	$4,000	Moderate	25-30	$150	81
Weekend Craft Show and Concessions	36	$5,000	Moderate	25-30	$350	106
Weekly Breakfast With the Coaches	4	$500	Low	5-10	$25	23
Weekly/Monthly In-House Lottery	41	$7,500	Low	10-25	$100	119
Wine-Tasting Gathering	8	$750	Low	16-22	$150	31

Part I

Fundraisers Generating Up to $3,000

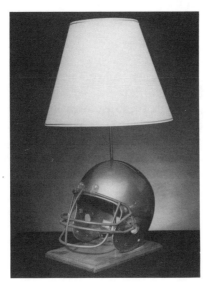

Fundraiser 9.

Consignment Sales

1

Potential Net Income
$150

Complexity/Degree of Difficulty
Moderate

Description
Although consignment sales are somewhat similar to sales in a flea market, there is a significant difference, which is that the items for sale do not belong to the sponsoring organization. Rather, the fundraising organization takes items to be sold on consignment and receives a percentage, usually 40% to 50% of the selling price, for items sold. Added profits can be created by the donation of refreshments (home-baked pies, cakes, cookies, etc.) to be sold.

Scheduling
The consignment sale, if a stand-alone event, is best held on a Friday, Saturday, or Sunday afternoon.

Resources
Facilities: Location, location, location—a good one is a must. The sale should be situated where there will be a lot of foot or vehicular traffic. An indoor or outdoor site large enough to display the merchandise as well as an area for storing merchandise beforehand is needed.

Equipment and Supplies: Display tables and informative and attractive signs are a must. Flyers, posters, a cash box with change, price tags, and a ledger (to keep track of who consigned which items) will also be needed.

Publicity and Promotion: Extensive, free media coverage will help spread the word. Attractive posters and flyers should be distributed and displayed community-wide. If this fundraiser is a tag-along event to another activity (such as an athletic event or recreation program), use the public address system to make frequent mention of the consignment items.

Time: The time required to plan this fundraiser is minimal (2-3 days). But it does take time and effort to actually get the merchandise together in one place for the sale. This can take 1 or 2 weeks or even longer. Plan on spending 2 to 3 hours setting up the items for display and another 1 to 2 hours cleaning up and putting away unsold items. The actual sale can take place on a weekend, or if it is part of another event it might be held at that time. The fundraiser could also be a regularly scheduled event, taking place every month, for example. In this case the collection of consignment items is an ongoing process and adequate storage space is needed to house unsold items.

Expenditures: This fundraiser can be implemented for less than $35. No expenditures are required other than the costs of creating posters and signs. Use of the site should be obtained for free, as should the storage area for the unsold items if there is to be another sale in the near future. Be sure to have adequate money on hand in the "bank" to make change for buyers. Also establish and publicize your policy regarding personal checks.

Personnel (Staff/Volunteers):   The entire effort can be staffed by 10 to 15 community volunteers.

Risk Management

There is no significant financial risk in this fundraiser because of the consignment arrangement. It is important, however, to maintain accurate records of what merchandise is placed on consignment by whom and for what asking price. Adult supervision of the money is a must. Also, any sponsoring organization should be held faultless in case of any accidental loss or breakage of consignment items. This can be addressed by having each person who leaves consignment goods sign a letter you prepare stating that the sponsoring organization is not responsible for lost or damaged items. This type of an agreement is no guarantee that you will not be sued, but it is evidence of intent and a wise precautionary move.

Permits/Licenses

A permit (such as a peddler's license) might be required and can be obtained from the town clerk or other appropriate municipal or township office.

Hints

Consignment items are collected in a central location for storage until the time of the sale. These items can be solicited from area merchants, businesspeople, craftspeople, and home owners. In short, anyone can be approached to place items on consignment. This fundraiser can be a repeatable event, held periodically either on its own or in conjunction with another high-traffic activity. It is important to solicit quality merchandise; this is not a "junk" yard sale.

Concession Stand

2

Potential Net Income
$250

Complexity/Degree of Difficulty
Moderate

Description
Selling food and drinks through a concession operation at athletic or recreational activities can be an ongoing, reliable, and significant source of money. This fundraising project requires extensive planning and careful supervision of a variety of individuals (youngsters and adults alike) who can be involved in a variety of tasks. The selection of an appropriate menu is a major concern. Pricing items so that the group makes a reasonable profit while not gouging customers is sometimes a challenge but is necessary for a successful concession stand. Confer with wholesale vendors to find out recommended prices for specific items and to find out which items are popular. Naturally, soft drinks, popcorn, nachos, coffee, hot chocolate, hot dogs, hamburgers, potato chips, candy, and cookies are all prime candidates.

Scheduling

Most concessions are tied in with other events such as athletic contests, musical recitals, and theater plays.

Resources

Facilities: Both indoor and outdoor facilities can be used.

Equipment and Supplies: The menu will determine the types of equipment the sponsoring group will need. Of course, cleaning supplies and water must be available. Many items can be rented, leased, or borrowed from wholesale vendors, including posters. You will also need various signs and displays; a cash box with change; notebooks for record keeping; paper towels, bags, cups, plates, and napkins; and trash receptacles.

Publicity and Promotion: Both point-of-sale advertising (signs and displays at the concession stand) as well as advance advertisements are necessary. Frequently, wholesalers provide advertising posters and signs for use in the concession stand. Advertisements over the loudspeaker during a game or event coupled with vendors who walk through the stadium or bleachers hawking their products can generate additional sales.

Time: Extensive preparation and follow-up are required for the successful operation of any concession stand. Planning and ordering items can consume several days, whereas on-site preparation can be completed within 3 to 4 hours. Cleanup tasks will involve at least several hours following the event.

Expenditures: Items for sale are purchased wholesale and resold to the public, and equipment and supplies that cannot be secured free will have to be purchased. Usually the concession operation can be kicked off for less than $200. Net profits from sales can be used to pay for additional inventory.

Personnel (Staff/Volunteers):   You will need 30 to 45 volunteers to successfully run a concession stand. It is essential that a manager or administrator from among the adult workers be appointed who will treat this operation like a business.

Risk Management

In many instances the general insurance policy covering the sponsoring organization will provide adequate coverage. However, a knowledgeable person should review the insurance situation. Sometimes booster groups and support organizations do not have the same level of insurance coverage as the recreation department or school they are working to support.

The mishandling and improper preparation and distribution of food can result in a nightmare for concessionaires. Great care should be taken to follow all health codes in the storage, handling, preparation, and serving of food. The financial risks of concession operations can be reduced by careful planning of the menu; it is important to offer items that customers will buy. Also, select items that will not spoil rapidly. Finally, do not prepare too many items so that you are left with 150 cooked hot dogs and no customers in sight. This requires prudent decision making.

Permits/Licenses

Depending upon the type of food and drink being served, it may be necessary to secure a variety of permits dealing with the preparation and sale of foodstuffs as well as licenses dealing with the type of equipment used in the concession operation. Contact the local health department and bureau of licenses to learn the specific requirements for your organization and location.

Hints

The key to successful concessions is to provide a good product and good service in a reasonable amount of time and at a good price. Choose items that are not overly complicated to prepare, that are highly desired by the buying public, that have a high profit margin, and that may be safely stored if not sold at a specific event. Gum should never be sold because of the cleanup problem it presents. Some concessionaires also conduct a sideline business in selling merchandise and sport memorabilia.

Renting Facility to Outside Groups

3

Potential Net Income

$250 to $500 per day

Complexity/Degree of Difficulty

Low

Description

A sport facility or recreation site is rented to an approved outside group for a daily fee plus evidence of adequate insurance. Such groups can include service clubs, swim clubs, church groups, square dance organizations, Boy Scouts and Girl Scouts, and operators of sport camps and clinics; the list is almost endless.

Scheduling

The facility or a portion of it may be rented at any time when the site is not needed by the school or recreation department. In some communities rental of such facilities may be restricted to nonprofit organizations.

Resources

Facilities: Any facility or site may be rented to another organization. Such areas include, but are not limited to, gymnasiums, swimming pools, classrooms, field houses, athletic fields, cafeterias, dormitory rooms, conference rooms, dressing and locker rooms, track-and-field areas, and baseball, softball, or soccer fields.

Equipment and Supplies: Specific sport equipment and supplies may be included in the rental agreement. Posting signs at the facility and mailing flyers to the community can promote the rental arrangement.

Publicity and Promotion: To spread the word that your facility can be rented if not otherwise scheduled, publicize in the local media, place signs within the facility, and contact (via mail or in person) various community groups and organizations.

Time: To accurately determine which dates are available for rental to outside groups, you must take into account the number of days involved in preparation for events and cleanup afterwards and, of course, be aware of when your own organization will be using the facility (including prep and cleanup).

Expenditures: None, if materials for the posters and flyers are donated. Otherwise you may need to spend up to $50.

Personnel (Staff/Volunteers):   It is prudent to have at least one person in authority present on-site at all times when the facility is being used by the outside organization; 1 or 2 trained volunteers or staff can fulfill this responsibility. A single administrator should be appointed to negotiate all contracts with outside groups.

Risk Management

A predetermined rental policy including a schedule of prices to be charged per day or hour is strongly recommended. It is imperative that insurance coverage be checked to ensure that it is adequate. If there is an additional expense for this coverage the cost should be factored into the rental charge. Managers of the facility should require at least a $1 million liability insurance policy as well as a signed hold-harmless agreement from the group seeking to rent the facility. A clear, comprehensive contract covering the purposes of the rental and the responsibilities and obligations of all parties will go a long way to prevent misunderstandings, disagreements, and damage to the facility. And, of course, requiring a damage deposit is a must.

Permits/Licenses

None are needed.

Hints

The on-site manager of the facility should walk through the facility with the representatives of the visiting group to go over all details of the facility usage including health and safety factors and the proper care of the facility and any equipment that will be used. For example, if a gymnasium is to be used there must be a clear understanding of what type of shoes are to be allowed on the gym floor and whether a tarpaulin must be placed over the floor prior to use.

Weekly Breakfast With the Coaches

4

Potential Net Income

$500

Complexity/Degree of Difficulty

Low

Description

A weekly breakfast is held at a community restaurant during a sport season. At the breakfast the coaches deliver a 5- to 7-minute synopsis of the team's activities during the previous week. The coaches do not sit at a head table but are seated at various tables throughout the dining room so those in attendance can visit with the coaches and ask questions. The breakfast is open invitation; those in attendance might vary from week to week and from sport season to sport season. Patrons order directly from the menu and are responsible for paying for their own breakfasts. The profit comes from donations, usually $5 per person per meal; a kitty is provided at the entrance to the room. At the end of each sport season the owner of the restaurant donates 5% of the purchase price of the breakfasts to the sponsoring organization. With an average of 100 patrons in attendance, the profit from the kitty can easily reach $500 or more weekly. The donation from the proprietor should cover the costs of the weekly meals for the coaches and other special guests.

Scheduling

The breakfasts are scheduled on Monday mornings around 6:30 or 7 a.m.

Resources

Facilities: You need a dining facility convenient to the majority of the potential patrons. The room should have a seating capacity of close to 100 and must be isolated or partitioned from the rest of the restaurant.

Equipment and Supplies: Sometimes a slide, film or video projector might be required for coaches' presentations. A sound system is also necessary. A promotional sign can be placed outside the restaurant.

Publicity and Promotion: The breakfast meeting should be publicized both as a promotional activity for the athletic organization and as a fundraiser. A professional sign can be placed outside of the restaurant advertising the weekly breakfast with the coaches. All in the community should be welcomed and encouraged to attend. Word of mouth is the best advertising possible. If the breakfast sessions are enjoyable and informative the amount of money and goodwill can be significant.

Time: This is not a time-intensive fundraiser in terms of planning. Planning can be done in a matter of hours. The breakfast itself lasts little more than an hour.

Expenditures: Minimal expenditure ($25) is involved because the patrons pay for their own meals and make their individual contributions to the kitty. Some proprietors may donate the breakfasts for the coaches and special guests in addition to contributing a percentage of the meals purchased each week.

Personnel (Staff/Volunteers):   Coaches, volunteers, and booster members are encouraged not only to attend the weekly breakfasts but also to motivate and encourage others to attend. A small but highly motivated and effective group of 5 to 10 volunteers or boosters can keep people reminded of the weekly breakfasts and hence keep attendance and profits up.

Risk Management

There is no financial risk in this fundraiser; similarly, the legal liability exposure is almost nil. The restaurant's own insurance policy should provide adequate coverage for accidents, food poisoning, and so forth.

Permits/Licenses

None are needed.

Hints

At each week's breakfast meeting a roving master of ceremonies can announce the amount of money contributed the previous week. This tactic helps keep the contributions high and reminds people that one of the reasons for the breakfasts is to raise much-needed money. Additional money can be raised each week by fining fans and boosters (and even coaches and administrators) for silly reasons such as being late, leaving early, having a birthday, wearing a unique tie or coat, talking too much, not talking enough, or having their names or photos in the newspaper or on television.

Selling Buttons and Pins

5

Potential Net Income

$500

Complexity/Degree of Difficulty

Low

Description

Personalized buttons or pins are made and sold to students, parents, fans, and other supporters. Various button/pin-making kits are commercially available that will enable you to create souvenirs or promotional items. If buttons are sold for a dollar profit per button, net profits can reach $500 per game or special event.

Scheduling

Typically pins and buttons are produced to coincide with specific athletic contests.

Resources

Facilities: No special facilities are needed. The buttons and pins can be constructed on a table in any room. They may be sold at the site of any athletic contest or organization event.

Equipment and Supplies: Button-making kits are available from commercial companies. Signs and posters can promote the button sales. When the buttons are sold at games, a booth or table and chairs, plus a cash box with change, should be provided. A notebook will be needed to record how many buttons each student has sold.

Publicity and Promotion: The buttons can be merchandized by person-to-person sales at the school or recreation facility and at athletic contests. Signs or posters in the community can also publicize button sales. You can make group sales by offering personalized buttons (e.g., "Downtown Businesses Support the Eagles in 1995") to people associated with organizations or businesses. And people who wear the buttons help promote additional sales. The sponsoring organization should have a specific site (in the school or recreation facility) where buttons are sold.

Time: Planning can take place in a matter of hours; 500 buttons can be made in less than 5 hours. Selling the buttons and pins can be an ongoing process with new and timely buttons being created all the time.

Expenditures: Most button-making kits cost under $50. Additional materials used in making the pins can also be purchased from these companies and are relatively inexpensive.

Personnel (Staff/Volunteers): About 25 to 30 volunteers and 1 or 2 staff members of the sport or recreation organization make up the manufacturing group and selling team.

Risk Management

There are no significant risks, either financial or liability. The kits and other materials you need are relatively inexpensive. If buttons for a specific date or event are made and not sold they may be disassembled, and the backing and the safety pin may be used for new buttons.

Permits/Licenses

None are needed.

Hints

The buttons and pins should be reasonably priced (providing $1 profit each) so that individuals will be able to buy different buttons for different athletic contests. Buttons should be created with the names and dates of events so they are appropriate only for a specific event. For example, instead of saying "Go Eagles—Win the Game," the buttons should say "Go Eagles—Beat the Wildcats November 11." Finally, special orders such as "Bobbie Says Eagles Will Beat Wildcats, November 1995" can also be filled, because the buttons are easily and quickly made.

Postevent Miniauction

6

Potential Net Income

$500

Complexity/Degree of Difficulty

Moderate

Description

A miniauction is held immediately following an athletic or recreation event. Donated items and services (performed by athletes, boosters, fans, or businesses) are quickly auctioned to those who elect to stay after the sporting event.

Scheduling

The miniauction can take place immediately after selected athletic events or recreation activities. This piggybacking onto another event creates an automatic audience pool from which to attract a sizable number of people, so the more popular the event, the better.

Resources

Facilities: The facility used for the athletic contest or recreation event can also be used for the miniauction. You will also need a storage area for the auction items.

Equipment and Supplies: Display tables are needed for the auction items, and a 3x5 index card is needed for each item. You will also need a microphone and speaker, a cash box with change, and a notebook in which to record buyers' names, their purchases, and the prices.

Publicity and Promotion: The miniauction can be promoted as a fund-raising activity that takes place periodically throughout the year. Because the more popular athletic or recreation events will draw more spectators, promotions for the miniauction should be aimed at these audiences. Before, during, and after the athletic event, the public address announcer should mention that the miniauction will take place immediately after the athletic contest and should describe some of the items and services to be auctioned.

Time: The miniauction can consume as little as 30 to 45 minutes. Planning for the miniauction and collecting auction items can be an ongoing process, although planning for the first miniauction can take 2 to 3 weeks. Plans must be made to store items to be auctioned. Total cleanup and teardown time will be less than 30 minutes.

Expenditures: There are actually few expenses involved with this type of auction because auction items are donated. Even the services of the auctioneer should be donated. Less than $10 need be spent in planning and conducting this fundraiser.

Personnel (Staff/Volunteers): About 20 to 25 volunteers and staff members are involved in soliciting items and services to be auctioned. Some of these volunteers can also assist in placing the items (plus index cards describing the items and services and blank cards for written bids) on the display tables prior to the game or event.

Risk Management

There are no substantial risks in this fundraiser other than failure to obtain sufficient items and services to be auctioned. Volunteers should constantly be on the lookout for potential donors and items to auction. There is no real financial risk; similarly, liability exposure is very low. Of course, you always need to observe normal safety procedures whenever large crowds of people congregate.

Permits/Licenses

Check with the local municipal bureau of licenses to see if a permit is needed to hold the auction.

Hints

Set up a display table in the facility before the event begins so that as individuals enter the facility they can view, read about, and submit a written bid on the auction items or services. Next to each auction item place a card with space for individuals to write their names and bids. After the athletic or recreation event is over the miniauction begins almost immediately. It is important that not too much time elapse between the end of the event and the start of the miniauction, or else the audience will begin to evaporate and interest will wane. The highest written bid on each auction item card is the beginning bid for that item and becomes the winning bid if no higher bid is received during the miniauction.

Car Wash

7

Potential Net Income

$600

Complexity/Degree of Difficulty

Low

Description

Volunteers gather at an appropriate location and set up a temporary car wash where drivers will be solicited to have their vehicles washed. Sites such as fire stations, convenience stores, or service stations are suitable. Also, parking lots adjacent to shopping malls are ideal, as long as adequate water is available.

Scheduling

Schedule the car wash on a Saturday morning or afternoon during warm weather. Pick a location where there will be heavy vehicular traffic, because business will depend, for the most part, upon impulse decisions by drive-by customers.

Resources

Facilities: Location is the key; the car wash should be in a high-traffic area.

Equipment and Supplies: Water, soap, buckets, brushes, towels, trash receptacles, and other items will be needed to adequately clean vehicles. Signs can be used to grab the attention of passersby, and a table can be set up at the site with materials highlighting the group's background. A fishbowl or cash box (with change) can be used to collect money.

Publicity and Promotion: Advance publicity is a must. Efforts to obtain free mention in newspapers and on the radio can reap big dividends. However, don't overlook the impact of "street advertising," that is, having youngsters and adults stand on the sidewalks with attractive signs publicizing the car wash, its price, the sponsoring group, and the worthwhile purpose for which the money will be spent.

Time: Planning and organizing will take as long as 3 to 5 days. Plan to spend 4 to 5 hours actually washing the vehicles. Have the volunteers and staff arrive on the site at least 1 hour prior to the starting time to get organized.

Expenditures: A minimal cash outlay is required—less than $25. Most of the washing and sign materials can be donated by the volunteers.

Personnel (Staff/Volunteers): Volunteers are the key to this fundraiser; 30 to 40 youngsters and adults and 1 or 2 professional staff (donating their time) should be actively involved in the on-site washing and the advertising activities. The ratio of adults to youngsters should be approximately 1:8 for ease of supervision. Adults should be the contact persons to obtain permission to use a particular site for a car wash.

Risk Management

Ensure that youngsters carrying the signs announcing the car wash do not stand in or dart into the street. Adult supervision is essential in the actual car-washing activity to minimize the likelihood that the youngsters will damage any vehicles. Although all concerned want to have a good time, no horseplay should be permitted. Obviously, there is little, if any, financial risk in this fundraiser. In terms of liability insurance, check to be sure that the site owner's policy will cover this activity.

Permits/Licenses

Contact the town clerk's office to see if a special permit such as a transient retail business license is required to hold the car wash. Also, alert the local police to the potential increased traffic flow or congestion around the site of the car wash.

Hints

Be sure to have adults at the car wash who will supervise and inspect each vehicle as it is washed. Don't let any vehicle leave the wash area if the driver is not completely satisfied. Ask the driver, "Didn't we do a great job? If not, just let us know and we will go at it again." Also, if detail work is done on vehicles, schedule 8 to 10 individuals on each car and charge $10 to $15 per vehicle. You may want to charge a price differential for vans ($3) and pickup trucks ($3.50). Finally, have a table, "fishbowl," and appropriate signs situated where the drivers park; the signs should highlight the achievements of the sponsoring group, illustrate how the money will be spent, and indicate that additional donations would be appreciated. You can also give away free pizza slices (donated by a local pizzeria) to each driver, but be sure to check to see if your community requires a permit or license to distribute food to customers and pay attention to health regulations that govern the handling of food.

Wine-Tasting Gathering

8

Potential Net Income

$750

Complexity/Degree of Difficulty

Low

Description

Members of the general public as well as supporters of the athletic or recreation organization are invited to a special wine tasting. Four to eight different kinds of white wine are provided; bottles of the wine are displayed on tables for the guests to sample. The wine selected may be from a single country or may represent different countries. A wine expert is present to lead the guests in sampling the various wines and to provide some background information (perhaps involving a videotape or slides) about wine tasting, about wines in general, and about the wines provided during the wine tasting. Additionally, fruit, cheeses, and coffee are provided. Tickets to attend the event can be sold in advance for $30 per couple ($15 per person) or whatever the market will bear.

Scheduling

The wine-tasting gathering can be scheduled for either a Saturday afternoon or a Friday or Saturday evening.

Resources

Facilities: The facility should be large enough to accommodate the expected crowd. If over 100 individuals are expected it may be prudent to hold the event in a spacious area such as a recreation or school facility. Or, space in a restaurant might be donated to the sponsoring group for this event. If only 25 to 35 people are expected this event could be held at someone's home—either inside or in the garden.

Equipment and Supplies: An appropriate selection of wines, cheeses, and fruit; coffee; disposable cups and stemmed wine glasses; platters for the cheese and fruit; napkins; and postage, invitations, and tickets are required. If a video or slides are to be shown, the appropriate audiovisual projection machine must be obtained in addition to the slides or video. If photos are to be taken, a Polaroid camera and film must be obtained. Promotional flyers and posters can be used.

Publicity and Promotion: Person-to-person contact is the basis of promoting this event and selling advance tickets, although tickets also can be sold via local merchants. An extensive publicity and advertising campaign should be undertaken, including the display of posters, mentions in area media, announcements at athletic or recreational events, and the mailing of flyers to boosters and friends of the organization. If invitations are used, they should be of exquisite quality, both in terms of printing and in terms of the paper used (embossed), befitting wine tasting.

Time: Planning this event can take 2 to 4 days. Obtaining the materials for the event may take a week. Advertising efforts should be completed within 3 or 4 weeks. Plan to spend 2 or 3 hours setting up the facility on the day of the event. The actual wine-tasting event need not extend beyond 3 hours. Cleanup of the site following the event will take only 1 or 2 hours.

Expenditures: If the invitations, wine, cheeses, fruit, and coffee are not donated, you will need to purchase these items. Similarly, there will be expenses if the site of the event cannot be obtained free or if it is necessary to pay the wine expert. Expect to spend about $150 for edible items as well as for publicity and promotion.

Personnel (Staff/Volunteers):   One or two staff members of the sponsoring organization and 15 to 20 volunteers will need to network to sell the necessary number of advance tickets. These volunteers will also be needed to secure the wine and food, find a suitable site, and prepare the site for the wine-tasting event. The presence of a wine expert is essential, because such an individual is able to lend credibility and enhance the enjoyment of the affair. Frequently, a knowledgeable person from an area vineyard will be willing to take part. Sometimes there are wine connoisseurs in the community who will volunteer to assist such a worthy cause.

Risk Management

The biggest risk centers around the ability to sell advance tickets. Sufficient tickets should be sold to boosters and staff to ensure that the event is on sound financial footing even before the kickoff of ticket sales to the general public. The major liability exposure rests in the possibility that the food or wine might be tainted, with those in attendance becoming sick as a result. Keeping a close eye on the preparation and storage of food and drink will keep this a safe and fun event. The risk of a patron becoming intoxicated is minimal. However, good public relations dictates that participants be made aware that the organization will provide free transportation home.

Permits/Licenses

Check with the local city hall or town clerk to see if any permits need to be secured for the preparation and serving of wine and food. Determine if a special permit is needed in your community to serve alcohol.

Hints

You must be able to secure interesting, high-quality, and representative wines if the event is to be enjoyable and successful. This is where the services of a wine connoisseur become indispensable. Similarly, the fact that the wine expert can share interesting facts about wines in general and especially about those that are being tasted makes for a truly successful and talked-about event. Volunteers can take Polaroid pictures of individual guests talking with the expert or with other friends and then give these to the guests as meaningful souvenirs of the fundraising project.

Marketing Second-Hand Sport Helmets

9

Potential Net Income

$1,000 annually

Complexity/Degree of Difficulty

Low

Description

Football, ice hockey, lacrosse, softball, and baseball batting helmets that can no longer safely be used by athletes are converted into table lamps, full standing lamps, or wall plaques for sale to fans, supporters, and boosters of the sport or recreation organization. The price of the lamps with engraved metal plates can range from $85 to $100 each. Helmet plaques, consisting of one half of a helmet attached to a walnut plaque, also with an engraved metal plate, can sell for $35 to $50.

Scheduling

The sale of the finished product can be organized around a stand-alone sales campaign or can be piggy-backed with some other event such as an athletic contest, a food event, or a raffle.

Resources

Facilities: Access is needed to a facility that contains an electric saw for the cutting of the helmets and the construction of the bases of the lamps and plaques.

Equipment and Supplies: Old sport helmets are the essential ingredients. Some schools may have 10 to 25 or more unusable helmets each year. Other items such as walnut plaques, oak or mahogany wood bases, lamp shades, electrical components, an appropriate paint and finish, and engraved metal plates will have to be obtained through donations or purchased at full or reduced cost. A helmet sawed in half can be used to create two plaques. Lamps will require the use of a complete helmet. Display the materials on a table during athletic contests and promote their sales on the public address system.

Publicity and Promotion: Extensive advance publicity can go a long way to give the selling campaign the exposure it needs. During contests or special events use the public address system to publicize the availability of the souvenir items. Also, display the finished lamps or plaques on a table at a visible location during games.

Time: This fundraiser does not require much planning; it can be off and running with less than 4 hours of planning. A helmet can be converted to a finished lamp in less than an hour; 50 lamps could be made in 5 hours if 10 people are creating them.

Expenditures: Expenses revolve around the components of the lamps and plaques, usually $7.50 per item or less. Initial seed money will be less than $75. Ideally, the work on the helmets will be donated by supporters or members of the school's shop class.

Personnel (Staff/Volunteers):   About 5 to 10 volunteers can convert the helmets and help market, advertise, and sell the lamps and plaques.

Risk Management

There is always risk involved in the use of power tools. Only adults or students under adult supervision should be allowed to operate saws and other dangerous machinery or wire the finished lamps. Also, the lamps must be safe to use, and thus a qualified person should inspect each finished lamp to ensure that the electrical components are properly assembled. The financial risks are minimal because the helmets are free and the components are inexpensive (possibly free); the labor to make the items should be donated.

Permits/Licenses

Depending on how the items are to be marketed some communities may require you to obtain a permit to sell the plaques and lamps. Check with the town clerk in the town where the items are to be sold to see if a business permit or peddler's license is necessary.

Hints

The finished products can also be used as awards to honor athletes and faithful supporters. In this event, the awards are given to the recipients at a public event so that exposure to the overall program and the efforts of the sponsoring group are enhanced. Displaying perfect examples of the finished lamps and plaques in the school and in prominent businesses in the community helps to make the public aware of the souvenirs and where they may be purchased. This method of generating money from unusable protective headwear can be an annual effort and will go a long way toward helping to pay the replacement costs of such equipment.

Parking Arrangements for Special Events

10

Potential Net Income

$1,500

Complexity/Degree of Difficulty

Moderate

Description

Whenever parking is at a premium there is the potential for making money by offering to provide parking. High schools and colleges sometimes host large sporting events (postseason competition as well as special tournaments), which sometimes creates a need for parking large numbers of vehicles. Sport and recreation groups that are able to provide skilled and mature leadership in this area, for a percentage of the parking fees, can realize excellent return for their efforts. Frequently, high schools and colleges allow individual teams or other worthwhile area groups to take over the responsibility for the parking situation in exchange for a percentage of the gross profits. Thus, if an event will attract some 3,000 vehicles that will need parking spaces (at $1 per vehicle), the profit can be sizable indeed. Assuming a 50% split with the host school, the group staffing the parking operation still can net a nifty bunch of change ($1,500) for 5 to 7 hours of work by 40 to 55 individuals. At $2 per vehicle the potential profit approaches $3,000.

Scheduling

Schedule walk-throughs and drive-throughs to ensure that the parking pattern and the traffic flow are acceptable. If the site has hosted a similar event previously, attempt to examine how parking was handled at that time; repeat efforts that worked and change those that didn't.

Resources

Facilities: Parking lots and other areas such as grassy fields that can be used for parking are needed. Also, access to specific areas needs to be restricted to provide for better traffic control and to eliminate attempts to secure free parking. Signs can highlight the parking area.

Equipment and Supplies: Secure adequate safety equipment such as vests, hats, whistles or other portable sound devices, flashlights, two-way radios, and lists of emergency phone numbers. Ropes, stakes, and signs also may be needed to identify and separate parking areas from walkways and nonparking spaces. You will also need a table and a cash box with change.

Publicity and Promotion: On-site publicity centers around adequate signage to direct drivers toward the parking areas. Public announcements of parking guidelines in the media will promote this fundraiser at no cost. Advance media explanation of any parking guidelines should be widely disseminated. Also, publicize how the parking "donations" will be put to good use by the sport organization. One way to accomplish this is through strategically placed signs at the entrance to each parking area.

Time: Planning the project and conducting a pre-event walk-through and drive-through may take 2 to 3 hours. Training the workers will also take 1 to 2 hours and should be completed several days prior to the event. On the day of the event the volunteers and staff members arrive early and leave after all of the vehicles are gone and the facility has closed.

Expenditures: This fundraiser involves minimal expenditures other than those needed for safety. Even the costs of equipment and signs should be less than $100 if the two-way radios can be borrowed.

Personnel (Staff/Volunteers):   The entire operation can be run by 40 to 55 volunteers and professional staff. There should be at least 3 to 5 adults in supervisory roles. The exact number of adults necessary depends upon the layout of the parking area, the number of vehicles expected, the age of the youngsters who are helping, and the length of time involved.

Risk Management

Although no substantial financial risk is inherent in this type of fundraiser there are other risks worthy of note. Check with the owners of the property or facility (and your organization's attorney) to determine the liability exposure of those giving directions to and guiding the vehicles. It is suggested that there be signs or flyers indicating that the group is not responsible for damage to vehicles or the theft of contents. The greatest dangers are someone being struck by a car, vehicles colliding, or vehicles being vandalized. Have all parking staff wear bright, fluorescent clothing and carry flashlights. Adequately train volunteers and have them work in pairs. Adult supervisors should collect the money periodically and store it in a secure place so that individuals working the parking area do not carry large sums of cash. And adult supervisors, wearing bright, identifiable jackets and roving through the parking areas, help to reduce rowdy behavior and vandalism.

Permits/Licenses

Contact the city municipal office or town clerk to see if any permits or licenses are required in order to carry off this type of fundraiser.

Hints

Very young kids are not appropriate workers for this event. Rather, adult volunteers or high school or college students should be used. Again, plan for adequate training, close supervision, and the absolute prohibition of any form of horseplay or nonsense. Pure professionalism should be the norm. Be sure to notify the local police about the parking arrangements for the event, especially if there is a chance that regular traffic patterns may be interrupted.

Selling Sport/Activity Posters

11

Potential Net Income

$2,000

Complexity/Degree of Difficulty

Low

Description

This involves contracting with a professional sport poster organization to produce about 1,000 posters that are sold to the general public and to fans for $2 apiece, for a total of $2,000. These posters, which are approximately 2-1/2 feet by 3-1/2 feet, are generally split into two sections; the upper part is made up of photographs of individuals and teams and schedules of a particular team, school, or organization, whereas the bottom portion consists of advertisements sold by poster company representatives (in person or by phone). Some posters also include space for a 9-month calendar separating the advertisements from the photographs.

Scheduling

The poster printing company usually will request 8 to 12 weeks lead time in order to sell advertisements and print the posters. It is important to distribute the posters before the season begins rather than waiting until after the season is 1 or 2 weeks old.

Resources

Facilities: None are needed.

Equipment and Supplies: Photographs of individuals and teams as well as team schedules and other data such as statistics should be made available to the printing firm. A notebook will be needed to keep track of how many posters each volunteer has been given to sell.

Publicity and Promotion: Because the profit hinges upon sales, it is essential that adequate publicity be allocated to the effort. Each company that buys an advertisement on the posters should be given two complimentary posters to display in their places of business.

Time: The poster company will need 8 to 12 weeks to sell advertisements and print the posters. The selling of the posters should be completed within 2 to 3 weeks. Planning for this fundraiser is minimal and can be done in 1 or 2 days. Allow 1 to 2 weeks to collect photos and team schedules.

Expenditures: There are minimal financial expenditures ($50) in this project, and these are usually associated with the costs of obtaining suitable photographs.

Personnel (Staff/Volunteers):   Only 1 or 2 staff members are needed to work with the poster company, but a large number of volunteers (20-30) are needed to help sell the posters within the community.

Risk Management

One of the risks in this endeavor revolves around the selling tactics of the poster company. Poor public relations and a tarnished image can result if the company uses unprofessional or high-pressure tactics in securing advertisers for the poster. The second risk involves the distance between the company and the sport organization. Because a poster company may not be close to your school or recreation organization you may have to deal with the company long distance. However, most of these companies have their acts together, and the printing of the posters is based on a "boilerplate" concept; that is, the format and style of the posters are essentially the same for all organizations. There are no financial risks because the posters are delivered free to your organization, which must then sell them for a profit. Similarly, the legal risks are minimal as well and revolve essentially around the liability exposure involved in the selling, usually door-to-door, of the posters.

Permits/Licenses

Check with the town clerk or municipal office to determine whether a peddler's license or permit is needed to sell within the community.

Hints

Emphasize to the poster company representatives that a hard-sell approach is not to be used with the potential advertisers; indicate that you intend to confer with the local advertisers to see how they react to the company's sales pitch. The various poster-printing companies throughout the country advertise extensively with small colleges and even high schools. Check the yellow pages for firms in your area that provide this service.

Dinner With the Coach/Administrator

12

Potential Net Income

$2,500

Complexity/Degree of Difficulty

Low

Description

This event raises money through ticket sales by a sport or recreation organization to supporters and the general public for a meal with a newly appointed coach or administrator. Tickets might be sold for $25, $35, or $50 each.

Scheduling

The event can be either a dinner (Friday or Saturday evening) or a luncheon or even a brunch any day of the week. It can be scheduled for a local restaurant or held at the organization's own dining facility. The menu should be attractive but simple and should provide for a reasonable profit per patron ($15 to $25).

Resources

Facilities: A suitable dining area, with seating for 100 people, in the organization facility or in a public establishment is needed.

Equipment and Supplies: You will need to provide table seating for whatever number of guests you expect. You'll also need to print tickets and promotional flyers. Keep records in a ledger or notebook.

Publicity and Promotion: The tickets for the event are sold only in advance because the number of meals to be served must be firmed up several days before the event. Take full advantage of the media (print and air) in publicizing and promoting the event; you should be able to get significant free mentions because the event centers on a newcomer. Also be sure to promote the upcoming meal at other athletic events and at meetings of the sponsor. Placing advance tickets for sale and promotional flyers with area merchants will also help disseminate information about the event, the guest of honor, and ticket availability. The period of ticket sales should not exceed 3 weeks; almost all tickets that can be sold will be sold during that time.

Time: Planning for this event can consume 3 to 4 days. Several weeks can be set aside to actually sell the tickets for the event. The meeting itself should be scheduled for about 90 minutes. This provides adequate time for serving the meal (45-50 minutes), a formal presentation by the guest of honor (15-20 minutes), and a time for guests to meet the new coach or administrator (20-25 minutes).

Expenditures: This event can be initiated with only $100 in seed money for advertising and promotion. The cost of the meal will be covered by the advance ticket sales.

Personnel (Staff/Volunteers): Approximately 30 to 40 volunteers and 1 to 3 staff members should form the core of the selling team. Person-to-person contacts are essential in ensuring adequate ticket sales.

Risk Management

With extensive ticket-selling by volunteers and staff, there is no significant financial risk. However, no community could support such a fundraiser every other month, so it must be used sparingly. The success is dependent on the appeal of the guest of honor. Because of the sale of advanced tickets, the only significant liability exposure rests in the quality of the meal and the facility.

Permits/Licenses

If the event is held in a public restaurant, there is no need for a special permit (the owners would already have the necessary license). However, if the event is to be held in the organization's facility, you may need to secure a permit from the health department or the town clerk.

Hints

It is essential to host this event early in the new person's tenure. The earlier the better, allowing adequate time for planning and implementing all facets of "Dinner With the Coach/Administrator." This would not normally be considered as an annual event. Its uniqueness and appeal rest in the fact that a new, and hence unknown, person is joining the ranks—and fans, supporters, and other interested people have a firsthand opportunity to meet the new celebrity. This event, in addition to being a fundraiser, can provide positive public relations and publicity to the sponsoring organization.

Annual Garage Sale

13

Potential Net Income

$2,500

Complexity/Degree of Difficulty

Moderate

Description

This fundraiser is essentially a typical garage sale with a few extra wrinkles thrown in to make it highly profitable. The garage sale is held at the home of a volunteer. Additional money can be generated through the sale of concession items that are purchased and resold or that are donated (e.g., lemonade, soft drinks, cookies, cakes, candies, brownies, breads) and sold at a 100% profit. The items for sale either can be dropped off by donors at a central location 2 to 3 weeks before the sale or can be collected by volunteers and stored at their homes until the sale.

Scheduling

The ideal time of year for this fundraiser is spring, when people are cleaning out their attics and garages. Plus, nice weather brings people outside. The garage sale should be a weekend affair, held Friday afternoon and early evening, all day Saturday (9 a.m. to 6 p.m.), and Sunday until about 5 p.m.

Resources

Facilities: Any volunteer's home that is strategically located to attract a large amount of foot and vehicular traffic will suffice. Adequate off-street parking is an advantage so the main street is not filled with vehicles parked along the sides.

Equipment and Supplies: You will need card tables and other types of tables to display the sale items and price tags to attach to them. Paper cups, plates, and napkins will be needed at the concessions area, and at the exit area you will need a cash box with change and a notebook to record your sales. Materials are also needed for creating banners and signs to promote the event.

Publicity and Promotion: Prior to the date of the garage sale there should be a concerted advertising and publicity campaign; secure free mention in the area print media, and have volunteers distribute flyers and post signs in the windows of area businesses. On the date of the sale, banners and large signs placed along the road can be effective attention-getters. Adults can stand at nearby intersections with large signs promoting the garage sale (and providing easy directions to the site). All of the advance and day-of-event publicity should mention how the profits are to be used by the recreation or sport group.

Time: Planning time for the event, including collection of the merchandise, is approximately 4 to 5 weeks. You will need 2 to 3 hours to set up, and plan to spend 1 to 2 hours in cleanup activities later. The actual garage sale takes place over a weekend.

Expenditures: Minimal expenses ($25) are involved because all items for sale are usually donated. Some food and drink items to be sold for a profit at the concession stand might have to be purchased prior to the event. Similarly, materials to construct signs will have to be bought if they are not donated. Be sure you have adequate change in your cash box.

Personnel (Staff/Volunteers):   This fundraiser can be most successful with 2 or 3 staff members planning the event and 20 to 25 volunteers collecting the items to be sold and working staggered shifts at the garage sale.

Risk Management

There are minimal financial and legal liability risks involved. The owner of the site should check his or her insurance policy to ensure that coverage extends to this type of activity. When you arrange the merchandise for display, pay attention to pedestrian traffic patterns so there will be plenty of room for people to browse without tripping over each other or the merchandise. All items to be sold are donated and volunteers staff the actual sale; thus, there are no expenses for salaries or for merchandise. The only financial risk is that you might raise less money than you hoped.

Permits/Licenses

Some communities regulate and license garage sales. Where garage sales are regulated, contact the city or town hall to secure the appropriate permit, which usually is free or requires only a nominal fee.

Hints

It might be advisable to have the garage sale at a local fire hall or Veterans of Foreign Wars facility so as to have a greater display area and greater ease of parking, and thus attract more customers. Location and the quality of merchandise are the two key factors in the success or failure of this fundraiser. Also, you may want to establish a policy regarding the acceptance of local checks and post signs to that effect. At the end of the day, if your group does not want to keep the unsold items, they can be donated to an organization such as the Volunteers of America or the Salvation Army; contact such an organization ahead of time and make appropriate arrangements.

Installing Vending Machines   14

Potential Net Income
$250 per month, $3,000 annually

Complexity/Degree of Difficulty
Low

Description
Commercial vending machine companies are contracted to install various types of vending machines (candy, soft drinks, coffee, fruit, sandwiches) within facilities operated by the recreation or sport organization. Even coin-operated video games can be installed. A specific percentage of the gross profit from sales is given to the sponsoring group. Depending upon the number of vending machines placed and the amount of merchandise sold, the income to the sponsoring group can be significant, especially in light of the minimum amount of effort required.

Scheduling
None is required.

Resources
Facilities: All that is needed is a suitable location within a secure facility. Commercial vending companies can provide insight as to where machines should be located for the maximum exposure to foot traffic and maximum profit.

Equipment and Supplies: None are needed; machines are provided by the vending company.

Publicity and Promotion: All promotional activities and point-of-sale advertising signs are provided by the vending company.

Time: Many vending companies will want a 3- to 6-month commitment from the sponsoring organization.

Expenditures: None are required.

Personnel (Staff/Volunteers):   There is no need for volunteers to be involved; one staff member from the sponsoring organization can easily negotiate the agreement with the vending company.

Risk Management

There is really no financial risk in this fundraising effort. Likewise liability exposure is minimal because the vending machine company's insurance will provide protection against claims of tainted merchandise. There is always a risk assumed by the vending company in terms of vandalism but that is part of the cost of doing business via this mechanism. It is important that there should be a policy addressing money "lost" in the machines as well as how to report to the vending company when machines are broken or out of specific items. Similarly, your contract should stipulate that the vending company promptly respond to repair broken machines, for example, within 5 working days of the defect being reported.

Permits/Licenses

You don't need to obtain any permits, but the commercial company must obtain all needed permits and licenses.

Hints

Call other sites where machines are installed to find out what the going split is between the vending company and owners of different sites. Don't hesitate to negotiate the best percentage you can. Take care lest negative public opinion be created by the installation of vending machines or especially video games. If there is strong public sentiment against specific kinds of vending machines in the facility or against the machines in general, it may be wise to forego this method of raising funds. Finally, installing vending machines in areas adjacent to sites where athletic contests are held might create competition for the concession stand that operates on game day. In this scenario it is advisable to turn the fronts of the vending machines toward the wall or to simply unplug them while the concession stand is in operation.

Free Car Wash

15

Potential Net Income
$3,000

Complexity/Degree of Difficulty
Moderate

Description
This project involves providing *free* car washes. That's right; the car washes are free, and money is raised for the sponsoring organization through the solicitation of pledges. Specifically, youngsters seek pledges of between 10¢ and 50¢ for each car that they personally help wash. If a youngster has 20 such pledges at 10¢ each, those pledges will generate $2 for each car that she or he helps wash. If the youngster helps to wash 50 cars, the pledges for that person will total $100. If 29 other helpers obtain the same amount of pledges and if they also help wash 50 automobiles, the group will generate some $3,000, which is certainly not bad for a car wash. It is not unusual for a free car wash to generate customer traffic of some 400 to 600 vehicles in 4 or 5 hours if there is adequate space and a sufficient number of workers. Naturally, all donors should be encouraged to have their own vehicles washed at the free car wash.

Scheduling
See Fundraiser 7.

Resources
See Fundraiser 7. Also, you need to create and have printed pledge cards and informational sheets about the project to be used by youngsters soliciting pledges. Securing pledges should take no more than 5 days. If more time is allocated, youngsters probably will just wait until the last 2 or 3 days to begin contacting prospective donors. An adult supervisor will need a notebook in which to record the license plates of the cars and the names of the volunteers who wash them. Pledges should be collected within 2 days following the free car wash.

Risk Management
It is wise to set a cap or limit beyond which the donor will not be charged. The youngster might indicate to donors that he or she will not wash more than 200 cars, which at 10¢ per vehicle would be a maximum of $20. It

is doubtful that 100% of the pledges will be collected. If 80% to 90% of the pledges can actually be turned into cash, the event should be considered successful. For legal and financial risks refer to Fundraiser 7.

Permits/Licenses

See Fundraiser 7.

Hints

The primary motivational factor behind the success of this fundraiser is the worthiness of the sponsoring organization. The prospective donor will pledge because of a desire to help the group reach a specific, publicized, and meaningful goal. Preparation of a professionally printed pledge card is essential. Also recommended is a printed information sheet or card concisely explaining how the free car wash works, the purpose of the sponsoring group, and ways the money will be used. This helps show the potential donors that this event is on the up and up and thus serves as a selling tool. Also, publicizing the fact that adults will be at the car wash to ensure that each vehicle is properly cleaned is an essential part of marketing this event. Finally, after the event is concluded and contributions are being collected by each youngster, the donor should be provided with a list (signed by an adult supervisor of the group) of specific vehicles along with their license plates that were washed by that youngster. This reinforces the credibility of this fundraiser and also enhances the likelihood of a high percentage of pledges being collected.

Free Car Wash
Pledge Card

Springfield, California, Youth Sport League
Please help support our youngsters.

Amount pledged (per vehicle) _____

Name of donor _____

Address _____

City _____ Zip _____ Phone _____

Signature _____ Date _____

(Note: the maximum number of vehicles
to be washed shall be _200_)

Name of solicitor _____

Blue copy to donor
Yellow copy to solicitor

Sporting Event Buy-Out Nights   *16*

Potential Net Income
$3,000

Complexity/Degree of Difficulty
Moderate

Description
An area business is solicited to purchase all or a significant number of seats for a specific home athletic contest. The business then distributes the tickets free throughout the community as a promotion for that business. The advantage accruing to the athletic organization is that additional income (above what would have been anticipated through the normal sale of tickets) is guaranteed through the advance sale of this block of tickets. Additionally, if more spectators show up at the game there is a possibility of increased profits from concessions.

Scheduling
Any home game may be promoted as a special buy-out night. However, weekend games will prove to be especially attractive to family groups.

Resources
Facilities: No special facility is needed other than the regular site for the athletic contest.

Equipment and Supplies: This project requires tickets to the event and signs or flyers identifying the sponsoring business. You will need to secure contest and giveaway prizes from the sponsor.

Publicity and Promotion: The buy-out game should be promoted to potential sponsors as a family activity. After a sponsor has been secured, the game is promoted throughout the community (by the business and by the athletic department) as a sponsored event. People can secure complimentary tickets by visiting the site of the sponsor. And, the sponsoring business distributes free tickets to employees, associates, and other businesses with which it deals. The business sponsor will provide, as part of the agreement, appropriate signs to publicize the event and the partnership. Numerous signs and announcements at the game site mention the sponsor, and frequent mention of the generosity of the sponsor is made over the public address system during the game. Giveaways and contests before and during the actual game are conducted in the sponsor's name.

Time: Minimal time (2-3 weeks) is required to sell this type of sponsorship to area businesses if prominent and influential representatives approach the area's business leaders. The time allocated for high-profile promotion of the event is usually 1 to 2 weeks prior to the event.

Expenditures: Expenditures involve advertising costs and the creation of signs (to use at the place of business and at the game site) highlighting the sponsorship arrangement. Even with donated supplies and volunteers helping to create advertising and promotional pieces, plan on spending $100 per event.

Personnel (Staff/Volunteers): About 10 to 15 volunteers can help sell this concept to business owners and promote the event; volunteers can distribute tickets to individuals and groups on behalf of the business owner to ensure that there will be fans to take advantage of the free tickets.

Risk Management

The greatest risk is that people will not take advantage of the free tickets and attend the game. To prevent this worst-case scenario, distribute many more free tickets than you expect people to use. For example, if a baseball facility seats some 1,500 spectators, then perhaps 4,000 to 6,000 tickets should be given to the sponsor for distribution to ensure that at least 1,000 or 1,500 people show up. Of course, if 6,000 show up, you have a problem. Common sense and a look at past attendance records will dictate the number of free tickets you should give to the sponsor for free distribution. Distribution of the free tickets to Boy Scout and Girl Scout groups and to entire classes in area elementary and high schools will also help increase the number of spectators. There is little financial risk in this fundraiser, and the legal liability exposure is also minimal. However, it is important that any objects to be given away to youngsters at the game be safe. You do not want to give young children objects with loose pieces that might be swallowed or with sharp points that could damage an eye.

Permits/Licenses

None are needed.

Hints

A team might be able to market several or all home games into special buy-out nights to area businesses. A team that averages some 3,000 spectators per game, yet has a facility that seats 5,000 people, could easily distribute upwards of 7,000 to 8,000 free tickets on behalf of the sponsor, with the anticipation of actually attracting a near-capacity crowd.

Mums for Sale

17

Potential Net Income

$3,000

Complexity/Degree of Difficulty

Moderate

Description

Mums are sold throughout the community by youngsters, their parents, and other volunteers. These salespeople take orders and collect money for mums during a concentrated period of sales, and 10 days later purchasers pick up the mums at a specific location and time. The volunteers take orders for mums door-to-door and by contacting friends, relatives, and neighbors. Adults can take the order forms to work and accept orders from their co-workers, thus expanding the pool of potential buyers; however, these adults may be expected to distribute the mums at the workplace. It will be best for the volunteers to collect money as they take the orders; however, you might choose to collect money when purchasers pick up their mums.

Scheduling

The sale of mums should take place in the fall. Ideally the order taking should be completed by the first week of September.

Resources

Facilities: The only facility needed is a site where the mums can be distributed to buyers.

Equipment and Supplies: Sale-order sheets on which the sellers record purchases and small advertising flyers to show prospective purchasers are required. A cash box with change may be needed at the pickup site, and change should be provided to volunteers going door-to-door.

Publicity and Promotion: The selling strategy should be based upon two factors. First, the customer will obtain value for the money spent, because the mums are of high quality and reasonably priced. Second, purchasing the mums provides significant support to the sport or recreation organization, and young people in the community will benefit. After the sale it is helpful to publicize (via articles and photographs in the media) the successful selling effort and how the money raised will be used to benefit youngsters in the area.

Time: The selling window should be no longer than 3 weeks. It may take 1 week to 10 days to have the orders filled by the mum company. The time set aside for the distribution of the mums could be from 1 to 4 p.m. on a Saturday or Sunday.

Expenditures: A portion of the money collected when the orders are taken for the mums can be used to pay the wholesaler for the flowers. This fundraiser can be initiated for less than $100, most of which will go for advertising flyers and order forms.

Personnel (Staff/Volunteers):   This fundraiser requires 35 to 50 volunteers plus 2 or 3 competent staff members.

Risk Management

The quality of the mums must be high or subsequent fundraising projects by the organization will be looked upon with suspicion. Care must be taken to properly train the solicitors (both youngsters and adults) in sales techniques. No hard-sell techniques should be used. Financial risks are minimal, because the order for the mums will depend upon the number of mums actually sold. You must educate young salespeople about safety while selling. For example, youngsters should not sell at night or in unfamiliar neighborhoods unless accompanied by an adult. Also, youngsters who sell door-to-door must obey all traffic laws; impress upon them that they must not dart into streets or cross in the middle of the street in their excitement.

Permits/Licenses

A peddler's license might be required in some locales. In others, no permits may be necessary. Check with the town clerk or the bureau of licenses to see what is necessary in your community.

Hints

Some organizations utilize the point-of-sale concept with the sale of flowers rather than the take-order plan outlined here. That is, flowers are purchased from a wholesaler (at a favorable price in light of the nonprofit nature of the project) and then resold by volunteers on street corners (weather permitting). This can be an annual event, held on the same 2 days (e.g., the second Friday and Saturday in September) each year. If the weather is poor, selling the mums may have to be postponed until the next weekend. The point-of-sale tactic is significantly more risky than the take-order concept because the group could be left with a large number of unsold (but already paid for) mums. In this situation, it is important that a business or a booster of the sponsoring group agree to purchase unsold flowers from your group at cost and then donate the entire lot to area hospitals or other charitable organizations. Another way to approach the challenge of leftover mums is to select a single site near a specific high-traffic area from which all leftover mums can be offered for sale at a reduced price during a final selling window (3–4 hours).

Marathon Party Night

18

Potential Net Income

$3,000

Complexity/Degree of Difficulty

Moderate

Description

This fundraiser consists of charging admission via advance ticket sales ($5–$10) for an all-night party for area youth (middle school through high school). The marathon party night consists of a wide variety of activities including dances; card games, board games, and party games; and activities like volleyball and basketball. Several televisions and VCRs also provide opportunities for those in attendance to relax and watch their favorite movies, which have been rented or borrowed from a local video store. Additional profits are generated through the sale of food and drink and even souvenirs (such as T-shirts), all of which have been donated by area merchants. Finally, area businesses that agree to sponsor the event can donate equipment, supplies, and food as well as cash.

Scheduling

This event is an all-night session beginning at 6:30 p.m. on a Friday evening and running until noon the next day. Although there are no specific plans for the participants to sleep during the marathon, they are encouraged to bring sleeping bags if they wish to take a few catnaps during the event. Depending upon the size of the facility and your imagination, as many as 750 or more youths could take part.

Resources

Facilities: This event requires an indoor facility that offers opportunities for a wide range of physical activities such as basketball, racquetball, and indoor soccer. An area high school or recreation center would be ideal because both would provide sufficient space for athletic events as well as various rooms for smaller activities.

Equipment and Supplies: Athletic equipment (volleyballs and nets, basketballs, badminton sets) and a wide variety of games and game boards are required. Most can be secured on loan or as donations. For dancing there needs to be an adequate sound system, including a tape or CD player, plus tapes or CDs. Televisions and VCRs are also required for showing popular videotapes. You will need supplies for the concession area (food; beverages; paper plates, cups, and napkins; and trash receptacles) and a cashbox with change. You should also have first-aid supplies on hand. Permission slips for parents to sign and provide home phone numbers are also a good idea.

Publicity and Promotion: This fundraising event should be hyped as a sound social event, in that the youth will be indoors under adult supervision in a healthy, positive environment. Notices sent home with the youngsters will help sell this event to the parents. Posters and signs displayed in area businesses and schools will help hype this special event. Public address announcements in schools and at sporting or special events will keep the party foremost in people's minds. The whole event is publicized as a fun time lasting all night and well into the wee hours of the morning. Youth (and their parents) should be aware that there will be a wide variety of activities waiting for them, including contests of all kinds, all under adequate adult supervision.

Time: Planning for the event can take as little as 2 to 3 weeks. The actual time of the marathon is approximately 18 hours. Cleanup time can take several hours.

Expenditures: Very little expense (less than $150) is involved in this fundraiser since everything can be borrowed or obtained as donations, from the food (pizzas, hamburgers, breakfast sandwiches, drinks, and candy bars) to the VCRs, videotapes, televisions, stereo systems, souvenirs, and sport equipment.

Personnel (Staff/Volunteers):   About 20 to 40 adults are needed to supervise every aspect of the all-night fundraiser. This includes staffing the admission table and ensuring that participants don't attempt to leave the building and then return. There should also be a cleanup committee composed of both students and adults. A ratio of 1 adult to every 15 or 20 participants will help keep the activities and enthusiasm under control.

Risk Management

There is little financial risk since all resources are donated. Check to be sure that liability insurance for the site is adequate and will cover an event such as this. There is a danger that participants might be injured during one of the physical contests or games. Trained adult supervision in this area is a must. You should have a plan of action for treating injuries—having a nurse at a first-aid station is recommended—and should have the names and phone numbers of the participants' parents readily available. Some organizers require parents to sign permission slips authorizing their children to attend the party. Additionally, there is always the possibility of the marathon being "crashed" by young people who are not invited. Prior notification of the local police is strongly advised. That way, they will be prepared to respond quickly to your call for assistance. Normally, the adult supervisors will be sufficient to handle most incidents. However, having an off-duty police officer volunteer to be present part or all of the time can be a big plus.

Permits/Licenses

Check local ordinances (town clerk or the local city hall) to determine whether a permit is necessary for the concession stand.

Hints

Once individuals have entered the facility for the party, they are not allowed to exit and then return. This will discourage individuals from leaving the facility at odd hours of the night and wandering around town as well as discourage them from exiting to obtain liquor and then returning to the party. If a participant insists on leaving, his or her parents should be notified.

Part II

Fundraisers Generating From $3,000 to $5,000

Fundraiser 30.

Progressive Dinner

19

Potential Net Income
$3,000

Complexity/Degree of Difficulty
High

Description
Six home owners volunteer to serve portions of a dinner to guests who have donated $100 to participate in this fundraiser. Up to 60 people, divided into groups of 12, travel to each of the six homes where they eat a portion of the dinner, smorgasbord style. The meal is divided as follows. The first home serves cocktails and appetizers, the second serves soup, the third has the salad, the fourth provides the main course, the fifth features a cheese and fruit course, and the sixth provides dessert. Each of these stopovers takes approximately 30 minutes with the exception of the main course, which is scheduled for up to 45 minutes. Maps outlining easy directions to each home should be distributed in advance.

Scheduling
This fundraiser can be scheduled on a weekend; it starts in the early afternoon and continues into the late evening.

Resources
Facilities: The event requires six houses, where owners are willing to donate their time, their homes, and their expertise in preparing and serving food.

Equipment and Supplies: The home owners must have cooking paraphernalia and an area where food may be served smorgasbord style. Materials for signs, posters, and flyers are needed, as are illustrated maps.

Publicity and Promotion: The promotion of this fundraiser hinges around the fact that it provides three opportunities for guests: the opportunity to experience excellent food, the opportunity to break bread with interesting guests as well as the hosts, and the opportunity to help a worthwhile sport or recreation organization. Advanced promotions can be posters displayed in businesses, announcements at other special events, flyers distributed throughout the community, and free announcements by the local media.

Time: You will need several weeks to plan for this event. It will take 4-1/2 to 5 hours for the groups to complete the circuit of all six homes, exclusive of travel time. With 60 participants (traveling in groups of 12 for a total of five groups) it is necessary to stagger the groups so that the first group arrives at the first home at 2 p.m. and each of the remaining five groups arrives at the first home 40 minutes apart. Thus, the first group arrives at the first home for cocktails and appetizers at 2 p.m. and will finish the entire route some 4-1/2 to 5 hours later, around 6:30 or 7 p.m. The last group begins the route around 5:15 p.m. and concludes around 9:45 or 10:00 p.m.

Expenditures: The food may be donated by the hosts. Or, vendors can be solicited to donate food and drink (and perhaps even to prepare the food) to be served at each home. This event requires $50 seed money (or less).

Personnel (Staff/Volunteers): In addition to the individuals who donate the use of their homes, 5 or 6 additional volunteers per home are needed to help prepare and serve the food and clean up afterward.

Risk Management

This fundraiser has a low financial risk although it is work intensive, especially in terms of food preparation. Food preparation assistance donated by professional vendors helps in this regard. An additional problem to be aware of is that the homes should be in close proximity or the guests will spend far too much time traveling. Liability exposure is minimal; the home owners' insurance policies should provide adequate coverage in case of accidents. However, care should be taken to ensure that guests do not consume too much alcohol, and organizers should be prepared to drive home guests who have had too much to drink.

Permits/Licenses

Since this event takes place in private homes there is usually no need for any permit or food or alcohol license. However, double-check in your area just to be sure.

Hints

This is an excellent project in terms of creating positive public relations while providing a modest profit. The dinner can be planned to coincide with a holiday such as Christmas or Valentine's Day, with the food and decorations befitting the holiday theme. An interesting twist is to plan more than one progressive dinner for the same evening, thus increasing the profit as well as the work. For example, you can stage a Mexican theme dinner and a Hawaiian theme dinner on the same date. A final adaptation, suitable only in unique circumstances, is to go the exclusive route and accept only 12 to 14 patrons, who pay $500 to $1,500 (and up) per couple. However, the homes where the dinners are served are those of local celebrities. A personal tour of each home by the owners is included in the evening's festivities, and the food itself must be a truly unique culinary experience.

Merchandising Campaign

20

Potential Net Income

$3,500

Complexity/Degree of Difficulty

Moderate

Description

This fundraising project centers around the selling of a national merchandise company's products (e.g., Tupperware) through a special arrangement whereby the fundraising group receives a percentage of the dollar amount sold. This percentage can vary and can be as much as 35%, or even higher. Volunteers for the fundraising group receive minisales brochures and order forms to aid in the selling process. All orders are prepaid. Immediately after the campaign is over the merchandise is shipped to the fundraising group and the volunteers deliver the items to the purchasers.

Scheduling

This type of selling campaign can be held at any time of the year although nice weather can significantly enhance sales.

Resources

Facilities: None are needed.

Equipment and Supplies: Brochures and order blanks are provided by the company's representative.

Publicity and Promotion: Word of mouth is the best advertising for this fundraiser. Motivation to buy is based upon the value of the merchandise and the intrinsic value of the sport or recreation program that is supported by the fundraiser. Volunteers who sell will generate prospects by approaching their neighbors, friends, relatives, and co-workers.

Time: The selling window should be no more than 3 weeks; all that can be sold will be sold in that period. And keeping the selling period to a minimum will ensure that all sales volunteers will be highly motivated and enthusiastic.

Expenditures: Since all orders are prepaid by the purchasers there are no up-front expenses. Brochures and order forms are provided by the company.

Personnel (Staff/Volunteers):   An effective sales force is the key in this fundraising project; 50 to 125 individuals are needed in order to generate really big profits. Parents and their friends can prove to be a potent sales force.

Risk Management

There is no financial risk because all money is collected before the bulk order for the merchandise is placed. The legal product liability exposure is kept to a minimum as long as the products sold are of high quality and from a reputable company.

Permits/Licenses

Some communities may require a peddler's license for door-to-door sales, although that technique is not the most common selling tactic used in this fundraising effort (most sales volunteers will contact individuals they already know).

Hints

This type of fundraiser can easily become an annual event with both sellers and purchasers looking forward to the special buys accompanying the "Spring Youth Soccer Tupperware Sale." Of course, there are several companies whose products can be sold, such as Amway, Avon, and Lloyds Christmas Party Plan.

Selling Holiday
Window Decals

21

Potential Net Income
$3,500

Complexity/Degree of Difficulty
Moderate

Description

Selling holiday window decals for a 60% profit can be a relatively painless and effective method of generating significant income for a sport or recreation program. Several wholesale commercial firms sell sets of glueless, precut, plastic decals that cling to any glossy surface, including windows, acrylic boards, and plastic easels. These decals are quite attractive and come in a variety of colors and styles, including traditional holiday themes, alphabet lettering, and animals. Check the yellow pages in any metropolitan phone book to find such a company.

Scheduling

This selling program may be scheduled at any time of the year. However, planning the selling campaign around a holiday such as Christmas, Easter, Valentine's Day, or St. Patrick's Day is ideal. The decals are sold on the spot; that is, the customer can buy packets of decals directly from the salesperson.

Resources

Facilities: A central location is needed for the distribution of the decals to the selling team.

Equipment and Supplies: The decals must be secured from a wholesaler. Secure materials to make signs and notices to display in the windows of local businesses. A ledger or notebook should be used to keep accurate records of the sales. Appropriate change should be available to sales volunteers.

Publicity and Promotion: General announcements concerning the sales campaign and the purpose for which the money is being raised should form the foundation of all publicity efforts. These announcements can take place during recreation or athletic events. Also, timely articles in the newspapers and over local cable television can help spread the word. Giving away decals as prizes at athletic and at other community events can help acquaint the general public with the items. And, of course, displaying the decals on the windows of various businesses in the community, accompanied with notices detailing where the decals may be purchased, can be quite effective.

Time: The actual selling window should be restricted to no more than 3 to 4 weeks. If you plan to use the Christmas theme, the selling campaign should begin in early November. If decals with a St. Valentine's Day theme are to be sold, the kickoff of the sales campaign should be in early to mid-January.

Expenditures: Individual sets of decals will cost between $1.50 and $2 wholesale and will be sold at a price to generate at least 60% profit for the fundraising organization. If $3,000 in profit is desired, $5,000 worth of merchandise must be sold. Most wholesalers will require you to pay a deposit before they will deliver the decals. However, some wholesalers will provide decal sets on consignment, which allows your group to pay for the decals from sales. Seed money will be in the neighborhood of $50 if a deposit is not required and $100 to $150 if one is necessary.

Personnel (Staff/Volunteers):   The larger the group of sellers the greater the likelihood of significant profits. Typically, 50 to 100 people, including youngsters and their parents as well as boosters and supporters of the sport or recreation program, form the core of the selling group.

Risk Management

Try to find a distributor who will ship the decals on consignment; this will reduce the financial risk. Some wholesalers may restrict the amount of unsold merchandise that may be returned to them, in which case it is essential that you not overestimate what your organization can actually sell. The financial risk diminishes in direct proportion to your accurate prediction of how many decals can be sold. Similarly, the liability exposure is very low and principally rests in the possibility of youngsters being injured while selling the decals. Proper instruction in the safety aspects associated with selling will reduce this risk.

Permits/Licenses

Some locales may require permits for door-to-door solicitation or may restrict it altogether. The local licensing board or office of the town clerk will be able to provide information about required permits.

Hints

The sets of decals are not sold on the local street corner, nor are they sold exclusively door-to-door. Rather, youngsters and their parents and boosters of the sponsoring organization approach their friends, relatives, neighbors, and co-workers.

Donkey Baseball

22

Potential Net Income
$3,500

Complexity/Degree of Difficulty
Moderate

Description
There are several professional fundraising companies that provide donkey baseball competition. One such company is Crosby Donkey Ball, Inc., P.O. Box 458, Chippewa Falls, WI 54729. For this fundraising project, you contract one of these companies to send a team, including the donkeys, to your town to play a modified baseball game (using plastic whiffle balls) against a hometown team; all team members, other than the pitcher and catcher, play while riding donkeys. Advance ticket sales are the primary source of profits, although additional revenue can be raised through the sale of souvenirs and concession items.

Scheduling
The game is scheduled as a family entertainment event and is typically held on a weekend afternoon or evening.

Resources

Facilities: Permission must be obtained to use a baseball diamond or other suitable field, on which donkeys will be ridden.

Equipment and Supplies: Equipment necessary for a baseball game, plus whiffle balls, is basically all that is needed. If concessions are included you need to secure equipment to store, prepare, and display food items. You will also need tickets for advance sales and items to serve as prizes and giveaways. Such items can be funded by local merchants.

Publicity and Promotion: The game should be billed as family entertainment, a unique event that pits the hometown favorites against the visitors on horseback (rather, on donkeys). Also, don't forget to publicize the use of the profits from this event. Several promotional tactics can be implemented either before or during the game, such as different contests with prizes, or giveaways to selected groups of people in the stands. For example, merchants might be asked to fund a special "bat night," wherein a miniature bat is given to every child under 5 years of age. Or, each woman could receive a screen-printed seat cushion. Or, everyone wearing the home team's colors could receive a special baseball patch. The possibilities are endless.

Time: The time required to plan and promote the event can be as short as 4 weeks. The challenge is to select a date that is workable for the professional donkey baseball company and does not conflict with other events. You should contact the donkey baseball company 4 to 8 months in advance to select a date for the game. The actual time of the contest and related activities will be around 2 hours. Setting up can be limited to 1 or 2 hours. Cleaning up after the game will take about an hour.

Expenditures: There is an up-front cost for hiring the visiting opponents (including the donkeys); other expenses will revolve around the publicity efforts. Total seed money will be around $500.

Personnel (Staff/Volunteers):   About 20 to 30 volunteers and staff will be needed to sell the advance tickets, staff the concession stand, assist with the parking area, and clean up the field following the game.

Risk Management

Contact an insurance agency to investigate the need for special liability insurance. The donkey company itself will carry insurance, but it would be wise to have an expert examine the existing coverage of both the donkey company and the sponsoring organization and make a recommendation about additional coverage. Similarly, the donkey company should be able to provide a bond of sufficient amount and should agree in the contract to hold harmless the fundraising organization and the individuals involved with it, as well as the owner of the facility where the event is to take place. Of late, some representatives of the National Society for the Prevention of Cruelty to Animals (NSPCA) have been especially critical of the use of animals in any type of fundraising or promotional effort. Carefully weigh the pros and cons, the financial advantages versus the potential risks, before committing to this type of fundraising effort. With advance ticket sales, the financial risk is minimized.

Permits/Licenses

Ensure that all health regulations are met in respect to the transportation, housing, general treatment, and medical care of the animals. Contact the local health department or a local veterinarian to determine whether any specific permit is needed and whether proof of appropriate vaccination of the animals will have to be provided. Check with the local health department or office of the town clerk about health regulations, and about whether a license or permit is required for the concession stand.

Hints

The donkey baseball game can be scheduled as a stand-alone event or can precede a regularly scheduled athletic contest or recreation activity. As with any event of this type that depends on advance ticket sales, it is wise to arbitrarily select a cutoff date, at which time you can cancel the proposed contest without incurring any financial commitment to the donkey baseball company.

Coed Fashion Show

23

Potential Net Income

$3,500

Complexity/Degree of Difficulty

High

Description

A coed fashion show depicting a specific line of clothing is planned for the general public. Volunteer models can include children and adults. Admission (advance sale tickets) can vary from $10 per person to $25 and above, and additional money is raised via the sale of donated drink and food items such as cookies, candies, bread, coffee, and tea. Or, in lieu of the sale of concession items, you can include a buffet dinner as part of the evening's festivities—but with a higher admission price (price the tickets to yield $10 profit per person).

Scheduling

The fashion show can be held at any time of the year. If the fashion extravaganza revolves around a specific theme such as western wear or a wedding theme, then you might want to schedule the show during a specific season. For example, the western fashion show might be held in the spring; however, the show depicting the latest in wedding apparel might best be held in the winter. Typically, the fashion show will run on a Friday afternoon and evening as well as the following Saturday afternoon and evening.

Resources

Facilities: An open area, usually indoors, is required. Ease of parking is of great help. If a buffet dinner is planned, the event is usually held at a banquet hall or restaurant with sufficient space for the fashion show and the dinner.

Equipment and Supplies: Electricity, a sound system, and adequate lights are essential. Additionally, a stage area and risers or a runway on which the models can walk and demonstrate the apparel are needed. Clothing should be donated or loaned by local businesses. The restaurant or banquet hall should have all necessary equipment and supplies for the buffet dinner. Tickets and a notebook for recording ticket sales and loaned clothing will be necessary.

Publicity and Promotion: Advance publicity centering on celebrity models (coaches, athletics or recreation administrators, sports figures, or politicians) can generate a lot of attention and increase advance ticket sales. Free mention in area news media is possible due to the nature of the event and the purpose for which the money is being raised.

Time: Allow 2 to 4 months of planning time to attend to the myriad details involved in this program. Plan on spending at least 4 hours on the day of the event to get everything set up and ready to go. The actual fashion show will last 1 to 1-1/2 hours. If you opt for the buffet dinner, plan on it taking 60 to 75 minutes. Cleanup can consume 3 to 4 hours.

Expenditures: Keep expenses to a minimum by accepting donations or loans of clothing. Even the site for the fashion show can be obtained free or at a greatly reduced price. Securing concession items to sell can run up to $100 but will generate a profit as long as there are no personnel costs.

Personnel (Staff/Volunteers):   You will need 30 to 50 volunteers to model the clothing, to work behind the scenes in preparation for the show, and to sell the advance tickets. Getting local celebrities to serve as models greatly helps in promoting the show. Also, an outstanding master of ceremonies will make for a delightful and entertaining evening. Influential supporters will prove to be a boon in enticing area department stores to lend clothing and accessories. Beauty salons can also be solicited to donate their expertise in helping the models prepare for the show.

Risk Management

Financial risks are minimal—equipment and supplies are donated or loaned, and advance ticket sales further reduce financial exposure. Care must be taken to protect the items being modeled and to ensure that they are returned to their owners in acceptable condition. The blanket insurance policy of the host site should provide adequate coverage for the event, but have an attorney double-check to ensure that the sponsoring group is adequately covered.

Permits/Licenses

If you choose not to have a buffet dinner, but if food and drink are still to be sold, check with the local municipal or county licensing bureau to see if a permit need be secured. Of course, all health regulations must be observed whenever food and drink are sold or given away.

Hints

Publicly thank all businesses and individuals who loan clothes or donate services, equipment, and supplies. Some promoters like to combine the fashion show with other promotional or fundraising activities such as a raffle or an auction. Requests for additional donations, made during the evening by the master of ceremonies, can result in surprising contributions, especially when influential "ringers" in the audience make significant contributions and encourage their peers to do likewise. Finally, this type of event lends itself to becoming an annual affair with a new theme each year.

Pseudo Dinner Invitation

24

Potential Net Income

$4,000

Complexity/Degree of Difficulty

Low

Description

This is a make-believe dinner for which formal invitations describing an "out of this world" menu at a world-famous restaurant are sent to supporters and potential supporters of the sponsoring recreation or sport organization. However, there is really no dinner at all. Instead, the invitations ask individuals to "participate" in the dinner by forwarding the cost of the would-be ticket ($35 to $45 per couple) to the sponsoring organization. The invitations clearly state that this is a "pseudo dinner," and that, in reality, donations are being solicited for the sponsoring group. If 100 couples "participate" in this pseudo dinner, the gross profit can be substantial.

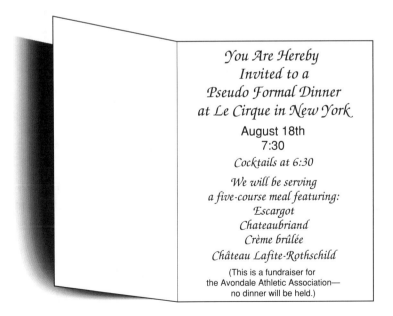

You Are Hereby
Invited to a
Pseudo Formal Dinner
at Le Cirque in New York
August 18th
7:30
Cocktails at 6:30

We will be serving
a five-course meal featuring:
Escargot
Chateaubriand
Crème brûlée
Château Lafite-Rothschild

(This is a fundraiser for
the Avondale Athletic Association—
no dinner will be held.)

Scheduling

The project can be undertaken any time of the year. However, planning it around a holiday season is a strategic move since individuals might be more generous and willing to support the recreation or sport program during this time.

Resources

Facilities: None are needed.

Equipment and Supplies: Beautifully engraved, formal invitations are needed, as well as thank-you cards or letters. A computer, appropriate software, and a letter-quality printer facilitate the creation of personalized thank-you letters. You will also need materials to create signs, posters, and flyers.

Publicity and Promotion: Since the whole fundraising project depends upon advance publicity and promotion, it is essential that influential volunteers spread the word among their peers that this is a worthwhile fundraising project. The value that people in the community place on how the profits will be used by the sponsoring entity will go a long way in motivating them to participate. The news media can be approached to periodically mention this "event" as a public service announcement or community news. After the make-believe dinner, the patrons (those who "bought the tickets") should receive personal letters from the promoters thanking them for participating in the "dinner" and commenting on how much fun everyone had.

Time: This fundraising project can be planned and implemented in as little as 2 to 3 weeks. The thank-you letters can be individualized and output by computer in a matter of hours.

Expenditures: The major expenses center around the postage and printing of the fancy invitations and postage for the thank-you letters. Additionally, various flyers and posters can be created for distribution within the community. Total expenditures should be less than $250.

Personnel (Staff/Volunteers):   A relatively small cadre of volunteers, about 10 to 20, can pull off this intriguing and profitable fundraising project.

Risk Management

This event carries no significant financial risk. The only other risk is that someone will mistakenly purchase a ticket thinking that the dinner will actually take place. To avert this embarrassment, state clearly on the invitation (granted, in small print) that this is a pseudo dinner and that no actual dinner will take place. And, if the name of a real, local restaurant is to be used on the invitation, be sure that the owner of the establishment gives permission and is aware of the true nature of the project.

Permits/Licenses

None are needed.

Hints

The uniqueness of this approach oftentimes works wonders with individuals who already are inclined to support the sponsoring organization. Thus, those individuals and families to whom the invitations will be mailed (or hand delivered) should be carefully chosen. To increase the effectiveness of the invitation, promoters can follow up with a phone call or personal contact. Variations of this concept include a pseudo dinner dance, a pseudo Christmas party, or a pseudo bus trip to the World Series or the Super Bowl. The pseudo event concept is to fundraising what the pet rock craze was to merchandising.

Ghost Marathon

25

Potential Net Income

$4,000

Complexity/Degree of Difficulty

Low

Description

A make-believe marathon, sponsored by your sport or recreation group, receives free advertising throughout the state (or even the entire country). The cost of participating in the marathon is $20, but no one actually shows up to run the 26.2 miles because it is a "ghost" marathon. Entrants, however, do receive a super T-shirt as a souvenir for their support of the cause and their "participation" in the event.

Scheduling

The ghost marathon can be scheduled at any time of the year. A southern Florida athletic or recreation organization might plan and promote a New Year's Day ghost marathon in International Falls, Minnesota, or Marquette, Michigan. Similarly, a fundraising group in a small town in Iowa might organize a ghost swimming marathon to be held off the coast of the Bahamas.

Resources

Facilities: None are needed.

Equipment and Supplies: You will need tickets, as well as souvenir T-shirts (preferably donated), with an appropriate message screened on the front or back, to give to (or mail to) the entrants.

Publicity and Promotion: Extensive media coverage for the event plus local promotional activities are essential. Ideally, the event will obtain extensive local and statewide (and perhaps national) exposure that will encourage a wide range of people to participate. The ghost marathon is open to anyone, regardless of where they reside; all it takes to participate is a check for the entry fee. Publicity releases, sent to news media throughout the state (and in other selected cities across the nation), should briefly outline the charitable nature of the event and provide an address where entrants should send their fees. Naturally, tickets for the marathon can be sold locally through area businesses and schools and person to person.

Time: Planning and promoting activities could involve 8 to 10 weeks, especially if the event is to receive extensive attention in the media.

Expenditures: Initial expenses will be less than $200. Most of the costs are associated with promotion and publicity, the tickets, postage and stationery, and the T-shirts. If the entry fee is set at $20 the net profit per person should approach $14 once the cost of the shirt and mailing costs have been paid. If the shirts are donated the profit margin is even greater.

Personnel (Staff/Volunteers):   About 15 to 20 volunteers form the core of the promotional and selling teams. The volunteers should take advantage of their contacts throughout the community to gain access to the media and to various businesses for possible donations and contributions (T-shirts, postage, stationery, flyers, etc.). Having a local graphic artist design and donate an eye-catching T-shirt design is a real plus.

Risk Management

There is no actual risk involved in this event other than the danger of being swamped with entry fees from individuals wishing to obtain the souvenir T-shirts with the catchy slogan. The financial peril is minimal, with initial expenditures limited to promotional and advertising efforts. There is no legal liability as long as the advertising is clear that the marathon is a ghost marathon.

Permits/Licenses

None are needed.

Hints

The concept of a make-believe or ghost event can be utilized with any type of physical activity. The attractiveness of the event lies in its uniqueness, in the attractive sourvenir available to the participants, and in the fact that a worthy sport or recreation program is being financially supported. Be careful when you publicize your ghost marathon lest some individual misinterpret what you are doing and actually show up for the marathon. The T-shirts will not actually be printed until the money is received. Wait until the checks clear the bank before mailing the shirts to the contributors.

Event Sponsorship by Businesses

26

Potential Net Income

$4,000

Complexity/Degree of Difficulty

Moderate

Description

This involves securing a business, organization, or individual to underwrite the expenses of an already existing or potential sport tournament or recreation program plus provide up to $4,000 for the coffers of the organization. Finding a sponsor for a tournament or special event should be approached from two angles. First, stress the value of the event itself, that is, its intrinsic worth and the benefits that accrue to those who participate and to the sport or recreation organization. Second, emphasize the benefits of sponsoring the event, such as increased publicity for the sponsor.

Scheduling

The scheduling challenge of this fundraiser for an existing event is to find a sponsor who can work within the existing schedule. For a potential event, the challenge is to select a date, time, and site that is acceptable to both the sport or recreation organization and the potential sponsor.

Resources

Facilities: Soliciting a sponsor does not require a special facility, but a facility to be used in hosting the event is necessary. Any facility appropriate for the event and capable of providing visibility to the sponsor will suffice. Areas for highly visible signs publicizing the event are desirable.

Equipment and Supplies: An appropriate presentation "kit" should be created with which to introduce the event and the organization to the potential sponsor. This kit should contain photographs and printed materials highlighting your group's mission and purpose, achievements, goals, and needs. Also, signs need to be displayed inside and outside the facility giving credit and exposure to the sponsor. A microphone and sound system are essential.

Publicity and Promotion: Be prepared to present your organization in a most favorable light. Why would the individual or business want to support your organization and your efforts? What has your group been able to accomplish? What are your goals and objectives? What benefits accrue to the sponsor? How will the sponsor's contribution and involvement be conveyed to the general public? Be prepared to toot your own horn if you have anything to brag about.

Time: Cultivating heavy hitters capable of underwriting complete tournaments requires time and patience. Set aside 3 to 4 weeks for active and simultaneous cultivation of many potential donors.

Expenditures: Minimal financial resources will be expended in courting a potential contributor, although meeting over lunch or dinner is certainly an acceptable approach. A professional-looking presentation kit can be created for less than $50. The cost of signs will vary depending upon the kind and number of signs; this cost is usually paid out of the sponsor's contribution. A good rule is to spend no more than 5% to 8% of the actual donation in acknowledging and publicizing the gift and in providing benefits for the sponsor. Total seed money will be $100 for this project.

Personnel (Staff/Volunteers):   Two or three professional staff serve as the sales team. However, it is imperative to use centers of influence to gain access to important decision makers who are potential sponsors. Obtaining sponsorship of a sport event or recreation program frequently requires sustained and persistent "selling" of your program and its value. The number of additional paid or volunteer staff necessary to organize and conduct the event will depend upon the nature of the event.

Risk Management

Be sure that you are able to reach the true decision makers. Find out which companies contribute to worthwhile local organizations and then cultivate selected individuals within these companies. The financial risks are minimal. You will expend time but minimal financial resources in soliciting sponsors. Money should not be irretrievably committed or spent for a potential event until contributed funds are received or a secure pledge is obtained. No extraordinary legal exposure is evident in this fundraising attempt although the athletic tournament or recreational event itself always poses a potential liability threat.

Permits/Licenses

None are needed.

Hints

When contacting businesses as potential sponsors be professional at all times; never "hard sell." Highlight the positive aspects of your group and emphasize the benefits that could accrue to your group as a result of the business's sponsorship and vice versa. Emphasize that the publicity generated for the sponsor leads to increased exposure among potential customers and, therefore, to the potential for more sales. Finally, be sure the sponsorship is worthwhile for the sponsor; provide tangible and intangible benefits in exchange for the contribution. For example, special benefits accruing to a sponsor can take the form of blocks of tickets, selected parking spaces, high-visibility seating; items of clothing (T-shirts, jackets, hats), unique premiums (pins, pens, patches), signs acknowledging the generosity of the sponsor, special mention in the printed program, or a plaque displayed in the facility, just to name a few.

Walk-a-Thon

27

Potential Net Income
$4,000

Complexity/Degree of Difficulty
Moderate

Description
Individuals participating in the walk-a-thon solicit pledges (from as little as 5¢ to as much as $1 or more per mile) from individuals and businesses. Individuals of all ages, from youngsters to senior citizens, can take part in this fundraiser. Plan on 200 to 400 participants. The distance involved in this event can range from 3 to 10 miles, and participants can choose to walk all of the course or any portion of it. Additional money may be generated from donations from the walkers themselves as well as from area businesses.

Scheduling
The event should be scheduled on a Saturday or Sunday afternoon during a season when weather will most likely cooperate. Nothing dooms this type of an event more than inclement weather. Have a rain date selected.

Resources
Facilities: The course can consist of streets, sidewalks, athletic fields, cross-country paths, or even an outdoor track.

Equipment and Supplies: Participants will need pledge sheets. Souvenirs (T-shirts, hats, or both) for the participants can be distributed at the start of the event. Tents can be provided at the start and finish sites and at the first-aid locations. First-aid supplies should be on hand. Refreshments should also be available so participants can replenish fluids, and trash receptacles should be nearby. Maps outlining the route and signs to mark the route are needed, as are materials for making promotional signs, posters, and flyers.

Publicity and Promotion: Each participant in the walk-a-thon receives a T-shirt or hat (or both) on the day of the event. In soliciting walkers for this fundraiser, focus on individuals who support your organization and its programs. Use flyers, media announcements, posters displayed in businesses, and announcements at games and other events to advertise for participants and donors. Of course, many participants will be athletes, parents, coaches, and people associated with the sponsoring organization.

Time: Allow 2 to 3 weeks for the solicitation of pledges. The walk-a-thon can last up to 4 to 6 hours. Promotion and planning can consume up to 2 months. The walkers who solicited the pledges should collect the pledge money within a week.

Expenditures: Minimal expenditures are involved. T-shirts and hats for the participants as well as tents and first-aid supplies can be purchased from or donated by area businesses and supporters. Plan on spending $150 to get this project off and running.

Personnel (Staff/Volunteers):   About 25 to 30 volunteers and staff members will be actively involved in setting up the course and managing the event on the day of the race.

Risk Management

The greatest risk in this fundraising event is to the health of the walkers. To compensate for this liability, you need to provide first-aid stations at appropriate spots along the course and to provide qualified medical personnel (certified trainer, nurse, physician, or physician's assistant). Financially, this fundraiser has little downside risk due to its very nature.

Permits/Licenses

If the course of the walk-a-thon is through the city streets it will be necessary to obtain permission from the appropriate municipal offices. In some locales the police department is authorized to grant permission and permits. In other communities the town clerk or the office or bureau of licensing must grant permission.

Hints

The success of this fundraiser depends upon both the number of participants and the number of pledges they obtain. Thus, it is imperative that as many persons as possible be encouraged to take part in this fundraising effort and to obtain pledges from friends, family, neighbors, and co-workers. Another twist to this event is to provide stops along the course where participants can go into a historical building, a garden, a park, a museum, or even a business to browse while resting from the walk. Of course a detailed map of the race course identifying all rest stops and points of interest should be provided to all walkers.

Peewee Wrestling Tournament

28

Potential Net Income

$4,000

Complexity/Degree of Difficulty

Moderate

Description

A peewee wrestling tournament for young wrestlers (Grades 1 through 6) is held under the guidance of the head wrestling coach at the area high school. A pancake breakfast for the general public is held from 8 a.m. to 10 a.m. on the day of the peewee wrestling tournament with the proceeds going to the high school wrestling program. Tickets for the pancake breakfast are $3 for adults and $1.50 for students. A concession stand operated throughout the day of the tournament is another significant profit center for the wrestling program. Prior to the tournament the high school coaching staff conducts a minicamp during which basic wrestling instruction is provided to all interested youngsters. There is no charge for the children to participate in either the instructional minicamp or the tournament. However, area businesses are solicited to sponsor each peewee wrestler to the tune of $50. When more than 100 youngsters become involved in this annual spring activity, the potential for substantial profits becomes great.

Scheduling

This event should be scheduled in March of each year following the conclusion of the high school wrestling season.

Resources

Facilities: The school or area recreation facilities (wrestling area, gymnasium, and cafeteria) are secured on a donated basis. The pancake breakfast can be run from the school cafeteria by volunteers.

Equipment and Supplies: Equipment for the sport can be donated by the high school wrestling program. Donated food supplies should be sought from area restaurants. Tickets for the breakfast must be obtained. Cooking equipment and supplies can be obtained from the cafeteria. If a concession stand is planned during the tournament, you need to secure appropriate equipment and supplies, including tables and chairs. You will need certificates, photos, or other awards to give to tournament participants and informational fact sheets for the parents.

Publicity and Promotion: The peewee tournament is promoted as an enjoyable experience for the participants and their families. The family aspect combined with the educational component becomes the key to the success of this fundraising event. Sponsors are obtained not only to help defray any costs of the tournament and the minicamp but also to provide significant money for the high school varsity wrestling program. Certificates of participation, photos, or medals are provided to all who are in the tournament. News articles and photos in area papers highlight the enjoyment and educational experience of the tournament and the minicamp and provide meaningful exposure of not only the peewee tournament but also the school wrestling program.

Time: The peewee tournament takes up an entire day. The minicamp is held Monday through Thursday from 3 to 5 p.m. for 2 weeks prior to the tournament. Planning can be completed in 7 to 10 days; however, solicitation of sponsors can consume an additional 2 to 3 weeks. Plan on spending 3 to 5 hours setting up for the tournament. Takedown will take another 2 to 3 hours.

Expenditures: There are no significant expenditures because all staffing, supplies, and facilities are donated. Concession items and the pancake breakfast food and drink items must be purchased if area restaurants do not donate these items. If not donated, the certificates, medals, or photos given to the youngsters must be purchased (at a reduced cost, if possible). Seed money to get this fundraiser off the ground will be $150.

Personnel (Staff/Volunteers):   Around 25 to 30 volunteers and 3 to 5 coaches are needed to run the tournament, the minicamp, and the pancake breakfast. These volunteers can be members of the varsity and junior varsity high school wrestling teams, athletic staff members, and interested parents and boosters.

Risk Management

To minimize liability exposure, arrange to have a certified National Athletic Trainers Association (NATA) trainer, qualified physician, or physician's assistant on hand during the tournament in case of injuries. Similarly, coaching staff members should also be present to teach and supervise. The preparation and distribution of the food and beverages should be managed by experienced, trained supervisors. Participants should be required to provide signed statements from parents or guardians stating that the youngsters have permission to participate and that they are covered under their parents' insurance, with the name of the insurance company and the policy number. Finally, you should hold a meeting with the parents and guardians at which time you (or your staff) and the coaches discuss what will take place in the tournament and remind those in attendance (both verbally and through the distribution of an information sheet) that wrestling can be dangerous and can result in injury. The financial risks are reduced through advance planning, the solicitation of sponsors, and securing of donated services and food items.

Permits/Licenses

A food permit might be required for the pancake breakfast and concession operations. If the tournament site is not a school or public recreation facility the owner of the site might be asked to assume the cost of any additional liability insurance coverage needed. If the site belongs to a school or a recreation department, be sure that liability coverage is adequate for the tournament.

Hints

This can become a highly anticipated annual event. The greatest challenge and the most work are in the initial year of this fundraiser. In subsequent years, once the event has been successful, the planning and implementation processes are much easier. The tournament itself is structured so that the participants (ages 6 to 12) compete against other youngsters their own size and weight. There should be at least four age brackets and at least 12 weight classes per bracket. Naturally there is a mandatory weigh-in supervised by the coaching staff. The advantages accruing to your organization include not only significant financial windfall annually but also tremendous goodwill on behalf of the parents of the youngsters and the general public. And, of course, the youngsters will develop increased skill in and appreciation of wrestling. This type of fundraiser can be used with any sport activity (gymnastics, volleyball, baseball, basketball, soccer, softball, etc.).

House Tour

29

Potential Net Income

$4,000

Complexity/Degree of Difficulty

Moderate

Description

A tour of 6 to 10 stately homes and mansions is conducted. The profit is made from a $25 to $30 admission charge, which includes a box lunch provided at one of the homes. The tour can accommodate 200 people or more. Those who buy advance tickets are provided maps to the sites and a time schedule. The guests, in groups of 7 to 10, will be scheduled to tour the homes at specified times (in staggered shifts). Each owner will write a brief description of the home highlighting its history, any unusual features, and unique collections.

Scheduling

The tour can be scheduled for a Sunday from 10 a.m. to 5 p.m. Weather is a major factor to take into consideration; the tour should be scheduled when excellent weather is the norm. In the event of inclement weather the tour is rescheduled for an alternate Sunday; this information is clearly communicated in all advertisements and placed on the tickets.

Resources

Facilities: Owners of beautiful and unusual homes that would prove interesting to the public must agree to open their homes to the public as part of the tour.

Equipment and Supplies: To protect carpets, roll-up plastic carpet savers should be used in high-traffic areas. Also, floor mats should be provided at the front door of each home to enable guests to clean their shoes prior to entering. Cleaning materials need to be on hand in each home to tidy up after each set of guests. Advertising signs and displays and decorations for each home need to be created. Maps, time schedules, tickets, beverages, box lunches, and a brief history of each home will be needed for participants.

Publicity and Promotion: Advertising in area media (radio and print), displaying posters in the windows of businesses, and distributing flyers throughout the community can pay big dividends. The day of the event, each home will have distinctive outdoor decorations such as balloons, banners, and signs to identify the home as part of the tour.

Time: Planning can take 2 to 3 weeks. The tour can last from 6 to 7 hours. If eight homes are included in the tour, this will provide approximately 40 minutes per home if the sites are somewhat close together and driving time is minimal. Five homes could be used and the time span reduced to 5 hours or less. Of course more than one group of guests can tour a home at the same time.

Expenditures: Expenses for this project include the box lunches provided to the ticket purchasers, roll-up plastic carpet savers, tickets, and advertising. Initial expenses usually can be held under $300 if volunteers prepare and donate the box lunches, serve as guides and hosts at each site, and create advertising signs, banners, posters, and flyers.

Personnel (Staff/Volunteers):   Influential volunteers and boosters need to convince owners of suitable homes to allow their homes to be used for the tour. About 5 or 6 volunteers and staff also must be at each home providing security, parking assistance, and general guidance. One tour guide to 7 to 10 guests will suffice. Also, the home where the box lunches are to be served (usually outside on a patio) will require additional volunteers to prepare the box lunches, coordinate their distribution, and clean up. Altogether, 30 to 60 people may be needed.

Risk Management

The greatest risk is of damage to one of the homes or its contents. Thus, volunteers and staff must be strategically positioned to prevent damage as well as theft. Expensive or valuable objects should be removed by the owners and stored for the day. There is minimal financial risk since the tickets are sold in advance. You might want to consult with a knowledgeable insurance agent about insurance coverage (in terms of theft or damage as well as legal liability). In most cases, however, special insurance is not needed, because the home owners' policies provide protection; to be safe, check with the owners of the homes.

Permits/Licenses

It is prudent to inform the local police about the house tour so that there are no unanticipated traffic or parking problems. If special parking permits are required, it's your responsibility to secure them.

Hints

Inclement weather will force the tour to be rescheduled because of the obvious potential damage to homes resulting from hundreds of people trekking through the homes with mud or snow on their shoes. The prime objective must be to protect the homes on the tour. This fundraiser lends itself to becoming an annual event if different homes are used each year. The consistent success rests on your ability to convince owners of interesting homes or mansions to take part.

Country and Western Dance With Lessons

30

Potential Net Income

$4,000

Complexity/Degree of Difficulty

Moderate

Description

An evening of dancing to a country and western theme is planned. In addition to providing a popular country and western band (or disk jockey), plan on providing dance lessons to attract individuals who are not accomplished western dancers but who would like to have fun and learn some easy steps. The profit comes from ticket sales. Tickets are priced at $35 (in advance) and $40 (at the door) per couple. A cash bar and the sale of donated goodies (cakes, cookies, candies, and snacks) can generate additional profits.

Scheduling

The dance and lessons can be scheduled for any Friday or Saturday evening, from 7 or 8 p.m. until 1 a.m. or so.

Resources

Facilities: This event requires a dance area large enough to accommodate 100 to 150 couples, as well as adequate and safe parking.

Equipment and Supplies: A band or disk jockey with records and an adequate sound system are imperative, as is an area with tables and chairs so participants can sit and relax when not dancing. You will also need appropriate decorations, door prizes (which may be solicited from area businesses), materials for posters and flyers, and supplies for a cash bar and concession stand.

Publicity and Promotion: All publicity should highlight the fact that there will be group instruction in country and western dance steps as well as opportunities for accomplished dancers to do their thing. Extensive publicity is necessary, including advertising in the media, display of posters in area businesses, and distribution of flyers via community pennysavers. Trade-outs (free tickets) with area radio stations can be made in exchange for free mention of the dance over the airwaves. Advance tickets can be placed on consignment at various businesses in the surrounding communities. Area businesses selling country and western merchandise should be approached to provide in-store advertising for the dance, to donate door prizes, and to purchase (at a discount) blocks of tickets to give to their customers.

Time: This fundraiser can be planned in as little as 4 to 8 weeks. Setup time can be 3 to 4 hours. The dance consumes 5 to 6 hours, and clean up takes another 2 hours.

Expenditures: Expenses include payment for the band (or disk jockey), drink and concession items (if not donated), publicity and promotional efforts, and site rental fees, if any. All together, you will need $500 in seed money.

Personnel (Staff/Volunteers): A qualified "caller" and instructor for the various dances is required. It is important that this individual show patience in working with beginners. About 20 to 30 volunteers are needed to sell tickets to their friends, neighbors, and co-workers in order to ensure adequate attendance.

Risk Management

The only real risk is in failing to attract a sufficient crowd to cover the expenses and provide a meaningful profit. Thus, a date should be set at which time a minimum number of advance tickets must be sold before final commitments are made to the band, the caller/instructor, and the facility owner. Securing a business, corporate, or individual sponsor can help increase the profit. The owner of the site should possess insurance that covers this type of fundraiser. If alcoholic beverages are sold, IDs must be checked, and organizers should have alternative transportation arranged for intoxicated guests.

Permits/Licenses

If alcohol is sold, the appropriate alcohol permit or license must be secured. Similarly, a food license must be secured and all health regulations followed if food is sold.

Hints

Attempt to reduce expenses by requesting that the band and the caller/instructor donate their services or at least reduce their fees. The country and western dance can easily become an annual or even semiannual event if those in attendance enjoy themselves and spread the word. Even those who are new to this style of dancing can be prime candidates to return to the next fundraising dance if they have a good time and learn a few new western steps. Of course, this event can work with any type of music popular in your community.

Pancake Breakfast

31

Potential Net Income

$4,000

Complexity/Degree of Difficulty

High

Description

A pancake breakfast, consisting of pancakes, sausage, coffee, tea, and milk, is the basis of this fundraiser. The breakfast sells for $3.50 to $5 (or whatever the market will bear) and includes unlimited pancakes per person. There should be a different price for children, perhaps $2. Popular music can be donated by a local or school band. A sports celebrity, perhaps a coach or a popular athlete, might stop by and say a few words to those in attendance.

Scheduling

The pancake breakfast can be scheduled the Saturday morning of homecoming weekend, just hours before the big afternoon game and other homecoming activities. This provides a built-in potential clientele, those individuals and families taking part in homecoming weekend. The breakfast begins at 7 a.m. and concludes around 11 or 11:30 a.m. Recreation programs or youth sport organizations can use different strategies by scheduling the pancake breakfast as a stand-alone event or to precede a special activity or game for their constituencies.

Resources

Facilities: This requires a large indoor or outdoor facility where 100 to 300 individuals can be served simultaneously, buffet style (400 to 1,000 during a 4- to 5-hour period). If outdoors, the event can be billed as a giant, extended tailgate party.

Equipment and Supplies: Items needed include the normal equipment and supplies associated with preparing, cooking, and serving a meal and cleaning up afterward. Tables, chairs, cooking equipment, food, beverages, and disposable plates, utensils, cups, and napkins are all necessary ingredients for this event. You'll also need tickets and materials for signs. A band and prizes are optional.

Publicity and Promotion: All publicity associated with the homecoming weekend should mention the fun aspects of the pancake breakfast and indicate how the money generated will be put to use by the sponsoring organization. The event should be billed as a family affair. There could also be a pancake-eating contest during the morning with prizes and awards given during halftime of the football game, thus providing additional publicity, admittedly after the fact, for the breakfast. Signs displayed within the community plus mention in the local media are especially helpful. Finally, advance ticket sales by volunteers can really make for a profitable fundraiser.

Time: Planning the pancake breakfast will take several months, including securing free food and drinks for the breakfast and confirming the use of an appropriate facility. A concentrated promotional campaign can be completed within 10 days, whereas the event itself is scheduled for 4 to 5 hours. Plan on spending 2-3 hours setting up for the event. Cleanup will take 1 or 2 hours.

Expenditures: If food and drink as well as the paper or plastic items are not obtained free, you will need to actually purchase these items, at a steep discount if possible. The donation of food, drink, and paper or plastic products is a big boon to this fundraising effort. If the breakfast is to be outdoors and a tent, tables, and chairs cannot be obtained free, then these must be rented. Solicit contributions from area restaurants for edible and nonedible items based upon the worthiness of the sponsoring group. This fundraiser can be initiated with approximately $250.

Personnel (Staff/Volunteers):   This event requires 5 to 10 influential volunteers to solicit free food, drink, and paper or plastic items from area restaurants, businesses, and wholesalers. About 20 volunteers will be needed to prepare and serve the food, and 10 additional volunteers will be needed to clean tables during the breakfast. Cleanup will be a significant portion of the volunteers' efforts.

Risk Management

Proper and safe food preparation is a must, and it requires constant, professional supervision of the food preparation area. This significantly reduces the liability exposure of the organization. In scheduling the volunteers, plan on the possibility that some people will not show up on time (or at all). Schedule more volunteers than you need; it is always easier to have too many helpers than not enough. If the breakfast is held outside, you should secure a tent in case the weather is inclement. Keep financial risks to a minimum by not spending cash for anything that can be obtained as a donation.

Permits/Licenses

If the breakfast is being held on school grounds or at a restaurant and you use the cooking and dining facilities normally used by the school or restaurant, no additional permits or licenses are usually required. However, if the event is being held elsewhere, food permits are necessary. Contact the local licensing bureau, town hall, or health department. Also, you will probably need to seek permission from the homecoming committee to host the pancake breakfast.

Hints

This breakfast, when scheduled to precede the ever-popular afternoon football game on homecoming weekend, provides an excellent fundraising opportunity and can become a popular annual event associated with the football game and other homecoming activities. Subsequent pancake breakfasts should reap greater net profits once the word is out that the breakfast is truly a fun experience. This fundraiser will work well around any type of meal that can be made quickly and inexpensively.

Selling Programs

32

Potential Net Income
$5,000

Complexity/Degree of Difficulty
Low

Description
A professional sport marketing printing firm specializing in the production of printed sport programs is retained to create and print programs for the sponsoring athletic or recreation organization. The printed programs include paid advertisements from local businesses and organizations; the ads are sold by the firm. The printed programs (anywhere from 500 to 5,000) are given free to the sponsoring recreation or sport organization, while the sport marketing printing firm retains profits from the sale of the advertisements. The sponsoring organization then sells the programs. If 5,000 programs are sold for $1 each, the potential net profit is $5,000. Naturally, the net profit will either increase or decrease depending upon the selling price of the programs and the number sold.

Scheduling

Since your group must have the programs prior to the start of the season, it is imperative that all photographs, statistics, records, and other data are collected and given to the printer well in advance. The selling of the advertising space should be completed 3 to 5 weeks before the printed piece needs to go to press.

Resources

Facilities: Some sport marketing printing firms request the use of an office or work space and access to several phones in the sport or recreational organization's facility for ad sales.

Equipment and Supplies: This project may require phones and office space to be provided to those selling advertising space in the program. Also, players' photographs and statistical data must be made available for inclusion within the printed program.

Publicity and Promotion: Generally, the organization is requested to provide to the sport marketing printing company a list of its vendors; this will form the foundation, along with names of local businesses and organizations, of a prospect list for advertisement sales.

Time: Usually only 1 to 2 weeks are needed to sell the advertising space. Add to this 2 to 3 weeks for organizing and designing the program and 1 to 2 weeks to print the piece. The programs can then be sold throughout the season.

Expenditures: The only expenditure is the cost of film and photos, about $50.

Personnel (Staff/Volunteers): This project requires 1 or 2 professional staff members to collect necessary data and photographs for the program and to oversee and approve the final draft of the printed piece. Some 15 to 20 volunteers sell the programs at various athletic events.

Risk Management

There are two major concerns in this type of fundraiser. The first revolves around the quality of the printed piece, that is, the appropriateness and accuracy of the contents of the program. These factors must be controlled by the athletic or recreational administrators or organizers. The second area of conern deals with the tactics used in the sale of ads. Be sure that the outside firm does not use unprofessional or pressure tactics in selling ads. There are minimal financial risks with this project. Legal exposure principally centers around the content of the programs in terms of appropriate photos and information.

Permits/Licenses

The sport marketing printing firm is responsible for obtaining any permits in the solicitation of advertisements. There are usually no permits required to sell the programs in your organization's facility.

Hints

It is wise to double-check on the selling/marketing tactics used by the sport marketing printing firm. You can do this by visiting or calling selected vendors and local businesses to see if they were satisfied with the way they were approached for ads. Locate a sport marketing printing firm by looking in the yellow pages or by contacting area colleges, which are frequently inundated with advertisements from such companies.

Celebrity Autograph and Photo Session

33

Potential Net Income

$5,000

Complexity/Degree of Difficulty

Moderate

Description

An afternoon session is planned at a local mall or at a recreation or school facility where well-known athletes, coaches, or other notables sign autographs and pose for photographs with the public. The money raised from the autograph-signing sessions ($5 to $10 per autograph) and photo sessions ($10 to $20 per photo) either may be split with the athletes or coaches (60% to the sport organization) or may all go to the recreation or sport organization. You can allow people to bring their own cameras with which to take photographs (cost remains the same), or, all pictures may be restricted to Polaroid shots taken by your staff members or volunteers.

Scheduling

The event should be scheduled for 3 to 4 hours on a Saturday or Sunday afternoon.

Resources

Facilities: A convenient location is a must. A mall is ideal, because literally thousands of people walk through a mall on a weekend afternoon. Ideally you can use space in a mall without cost. Impress upon the mall manager that positive publicity will be generated for the shopping mall by such a contribution to a worthy cause.

Equipment and Supplies: Several Polaroid cameras are needed if more than one celebrity is on hand. These can be borrowed. Don't forget film—lots of film (donated if possible). A professional-looking and strategically located booth will attract passersby. The booth can be built by volunteers if the mall does not already have such a temporary structure. Signs can be used to advertise the event. A small cash box and adequate change are needed, as is a notebook to record sales and income.

Publicity and Promotion: Three to four weeks of advance publicity in the print media and on the radio and free mentions on local television will publicize the event to a large segment of the public. Depending upon the popularity of the celebrities scheduled to be on hand, there may be extensive free exposure of the event by the media. Advance signs in the mall hawking the event, created and erected by the mall personnel, are great marketing tools.

Time: The autograph/photo session should not extend beyond 3 to 4 hours. Planning the event may take upwards of 2 months, especially when you must confirm attendance by celebrities.

Expenditures: If you cannot obtain free media advertising, it must be purchased, possibly at reduced cost. Similarly, the signs in the mall and the booth itself must be paid for if they are not donated by the mall management. Seed money will total around $150.

Personnel (Staff/Volunteers):   You will need 10 to 15 staff and volunteers to operate the booth, that is, take the pictures, organize the autograph signing, accept money, and generally oversee the event so that all runs smoothly. In approaching the celebrities as well as the mall managers, make use of contacts with "centers of influence" (influential people who support your group) so as to gain access to these individuals on a favorable basis.

Risk Management

Providing protection and privacy for the celebrities is important. Also, there is always a danger that a celebrity might be a no-show, which can be embarrassing for your organization. Remaining in contact with the celebrities (or their agents) is advisable. Also, you can send the celebrities copies of all of the advertisements highlighting their planned attendance to remind them that the event depends upon their presence. Finally, if celebrities are to receive compensation it is wise to pay only a portion of the fee before the event and the rest after the event. Liability exposure is minimal since the mall's blanket insurance policy should provide adequate protection. The financial risk is minimal if celebrities donate their presence because of the low start-up costs, but if celebrities must be paid the risk can be considerable.

Permits/Licenses

The mall manager will advise you of any specific permits required by the local municipality or township. Usually, no special licensing is needed for this type of event.

Hints

Even if the celebrities will not donate their presence, there is still a significant amount of money to be made for the sponsoring organization. Some celebrities will take a flat appearance fee, while others will take a percentage; see if an area business will underwrite the appearance fee. There are four essential components for a successful event. The first is the caliber and pulling power of the celebrities. The second is the amount of advance publicity and exposure highlighting the event. The third is the location of the session: It must be convenient to reach, provide sufficient parking area, and have a built-in population (such as in a mall). The fourth is that the celebrities agree to appear for free or for a very small percentage of the proceeds.

Generic Auction

34

Potential Net Income

$5,000

Complexity/Degree of Difficulty

Moderate

Description

Donated items are auctioned to the highest bidder. A well-run concession stand can be an added profit center.

Scheduling

Typically, auctions should be scheduled on Friday, Saturday, or Sunday afternoon or evening. However, the auctions can also be conducted at other times. The auctions can be scheduled as a stand-alone event or can be held in conjunction with other events. For example, successful auctions have been held before or after athletic contests or in connection with luncheons or dinners.

Resources

Facilities: This event can be held in any indoor or outdoor area that will accommodate a large crowd and provide adequate space to display auction items. Also, you may need a place to store the items before the auction.

Equipment and Supplies: A loudspeaker system, tables to display the merchandise, and chairs for bidders must be secured. A printed list of items to be auctioned should be prepared and distributed to those in attendance. Consecutively numbered signs should be given to registered bidders, and sales should be recorded in a ledger. Concession equipment and supplies are also required if there is to be this additional profit center. Flyers can be made and distributed before the auction to promote interest.

Publicity and Promotion: Advertising in area newspapers and weekly penny-savers will reach many interested people. Publicizing a list of the more popular items will also pique interest. Flyers distributed directly to homes throughout the area and posters displayed in windows of area businesses will prove to be most effective. Be sure to publicize both the items to be auctioned and the nature of the nonprofit group sponsoring the auction.

Time: Collecting the items to be auctioned can take from 2 to 4 months. Actual setup for an auction can take as long as 2 to 8 hours; when many items are to be auctioned the time to catalog and set up for the big event can take 2 to 3 days. Auctions themselves usually take 3 to 6 hours, depending on the number of items auctioned and the number and interest of bidders. Cleanup time can easily consume 2 to 3 hours; more time may be required if merchandise remains and must be moved to a storage space.

Expenditures: There will be costs involved in advertising. Also, you will have to pay for the auctioneer's services if not donated. You should not have to pay more than $150 to get this fundraiser off the ground.

Personnel (Staff/Volunteers):   A professional auctioneer and 3 to 7 accompanying support staff—hawkers, ring personnel, bookkeepers—are an absolute must; you cannot skimp in this area. The professional auctioneer, using the auctioneer's cadence, lends sophistication to the event and also can generate higher prices (and thus profits) for the items auctioned. You will need 15 to 25 volunteers and 1 or 2 staff members to solicit, collect, organize, and store the auction items. Additionally, 10 to 15 volunteers are needed to provide security and coordinate the concession stand and parking area.

Risk Management

Obtain liability insurance for the event if your organization's blanket policy does not cover an activity such as an auction. Check with your insurance agent to be safe. There is little financial risk because the auction items and usually the auctioneer's services and staff are donated. Many auctioneers willingly donate their time to "call" an auction for a worthy cause. The professional auctioneer will be knowledgeable about the laws regarding the collection and payment of sales taxes.

Permits/Licenses

Check with the town clerk or the bureau of licenses to determine whether a permit or license is required for the auction.

Hints

Anything can be auctioned, not just tangible objects. For example, athletes can be "auctioned" to perform yard work for 2 to 4 hours. Also, recreation staff, coaches, and sport administrators can be "auctioned" to have lunch or dinner with the purchasers. Free dinners or "great escape weekends" at local hotels, tickets to shows and theme parks, and items from celebrities can be auctioned. All auction items and the auctioneer's services should be donated.

Celebrity
Athletic Contest

35

Potential Net Income

$5,000

Complexity/Degree of Difficulty

Moderate

Description

An athletic contest, such as softball, volleyball, basketball, or soccer, is scheduled between the staff members of a recreation or sport organization and celebrities, such as professional athletes or radio and TV personalities. Admission is charged and additional profits may result from sale of concessions. In many cases the celebrities will donate their time and presence, leaving all profits to the sponsoring organization.

Scheduling

The contest should be scheduled to attract the greatest paying audience, most likely a Friday or Saturday evening or a Saturday or Sunday afternoon.

Resources

Facilities: The event requires a gymnasium or sports field or other facility, depending upon the nature of the sport contest.

Equipment and Supplies: You will need concessions equipment and supplies as well as any equipment or uniforms for the game. Programs, to be distributed free to those in attendance, should be created and printed. A loudspeaker system should be available. You will also need materials for making promotional signs, posters, and flyers.

Publicity and Promotion: Tap all of the normal publicity avenues (flyers, ads in local newspapers, radio spots) in an effort to reach as large an audience as possible. The two key promotional messages conveyed to the public should revolve around the enjoyment of the contest and the ways the profits from the game will benefit the sponsoring group. Since celebrities are involved many news outlets might publicize the event without cost as a public service message or even as a sports news item. An advertised autograph session preceding or following the athletic contest might certainly increase its attractiveness. Paid advertisements might be solicited for the programs, which would not only pay for the cost of the programs but also provide additional profit.

Time: The actual event takes 2 hours. Planning and organizing could involve as much as 4 to 8 weeks. Plan to spend an hour cleaning up following the contest.

Expenditures: If the celebrities donate their time, the major expenses ($200 seed money) will revolve around the advertising and promotion efforts, the printed programs, and concessions items.

Personnel (Staff/Volunteers):   Coaches and teachers at the school or employees at the recreation department are involved as players in the contest against the visiting notables. Volunteers are needed to serve as officials, public address announcers, statisticians, and concessionaires. As many as 20 to 35 volunteers and professional staff members can play an active part in this fundraiser.

Risk Management

The school, recreation department, or sport organization's blanket insurance policy should provide adequate coverage for this special event. The worst-case scenario is that the celebrity team is a no-show. To prevent this financial and public relations fiasco, make every effort (by frequent communication) to ensure that the visiting team indeed meets its obligation.

Permits/Licenses

The concessions stand must adhere to local health regulations. Check with the local health department or bureau of licenses to find out specific requirements regarding permits or licenses.

Hints

The key to a successful project is a signed agreement from celebrities to participate in the game. Since the popularity of the celebrity opponents will determine, for the most part, whether the fundraiser is successful, try to sign up the most popular celebrities possible.

Weekend Craft Show and Concessions

36

Potential Net Income

$5,000

Complexity/Degree of Difficulty

Moderate

Description

A 2-day craft show is held on a Saturday and Sunday in a large indoor facility such as an automobile dealer's showroom and repair bays or in a gymnasium or field house. Individual spaces measuring 8 feet by 10 feet are rented to craft vendors for $50 to $75 (paid in advance) for the weekend. Vendors, who may number over 100, provide their own tables, displays, and signs. There is no admission fee for the public and the vendors do not pay a percentage of their profits. Additional money is made by the fundraising group through the sale of concession items, some of which may be donated.

Scheduling

The event should be held during good weather even though it is indoors; fall and spring are excellent times. Schedule around other area craft shows.

Resources

Facilities: The key is the indoor facility, which should be accessible to the fundraising group from Friday afternoon to late Sunday afternoon to allow for setup and teardown by the vendors. If a school gymnasium is used there cannot be any other events scheduled for the weekend. If a car showroom is used there must be ample parking, which necessitates that the car dealer move some of the rolling stock to the back lot.

Equipment and Supplies: This event requires concession equipment and supplies, tables for the concession area, trash receptacles, and food and drink items to be sold. You will also need stationery and postage for sending invitations and a notebook or binder to keep records of communications and agreements with vendors. Of course, signs, posters, and flyers need to be created.

Publicity and Promotion: Advertising in state and area craft publications and local media, as well as using special invitational letters to attract sufficient vendors, is a must. Such advertising should begin 8 to 12 months before the event. You can obtain lists of names and addresses of craft vendors by contacting local artisans, church groups, and craft stores. Advertising for the general public to attend the free craft show should be carried out for at least 4 to 5 weeks prior to the event through posters, flyers, and mention in the media.

Time: Planning the event and securing commitments from vendors could take up to 8 months, if not more. The event is held from 8 a.m. to 5 p.m. on a Saturday and Sunday. Allow 6 to 8 hours for the vendors to set up. Tearing down the booths, tables, and chairs and cleaning up will take up to 4 hours.

Expenditures: Almost all expenses will center around advertising and mailing efforts ($250) and purchasing of concession items ($100) for resale. Much of the profits from concessions will probably cover the costs of advertising once the annual craft show becomes a fixture in the community.

Personnel (Staff/Volunteers):   You will need 25 to 30 volunteers to distribute advertisements throughout the community, operate the concession stand, and handle parking. There should be a coordinating committee headed by an individual who will oversee the details of all arrangements with potential vendors and the site owner.

Risk Management

Insurance for the concession area should be obtained. The site owner's regular insurance policy should cover the additional liability exposure created by the event. Volunteers who help with parking should wear bright jackets to be easily seen and recognized. There is little financial risk since the vendors pay the rental fee up front and the cost of concession items (those that are not donated) is paid from the concessions profits.

Permits/Licenses

Find out about local ordinances concerning food operations. Some communities might require a license for the concession stand as well as licenses for the individual vendors; contact city hall or the town clerk to find out about any special requirements.

Hints

This can easily become an annual event, with the number of vendors and the number of people attending the craft show increasing each year. Query the vendors, the site owner, and those attending the craft show to solicit reactions to the show and suggestions about what might be improved. Success breeds success.

Professional Wrestling Exhibition

37

Potential Net Income
$5,000

Complexity/Degree of Difficulty
Moderate

Description
This involves contracting with a professional wrestling organization to provide a series of wrestling matches in your community. Profit is generated from ticket sales; the sale of concession items and souvenirs (preferably donated) can increase profits. Sponsors are solicited to help defray the cost of renting a facility if one is necessary.

Scheduling
The matches can be scheduled on any night of the week, although the best nights are Friday and Saturday and the worst, Sunday. The fundraiser can consist of a single evening or two or more successive evenings.

Resources
Facilities: The key component to this event is adequate seating for the spectators. A municipal auditorium or large athletic or recreational facility would be ideal.

Equipment and Supplies: The touring wrestling professionals will bring their own portable ring and other paraphernalia. You will need to have tickets printed. An excellent sound system is mandatory. Inexpensive programs should be printed, and souvenirs purchased for resale. You will also need concession items, equipment, and supplies; and a cash box with change.

Publicity and Promotion: Advance publicity to promote ticket sales is your greatest concern. Use of a ticket-selling agency like TicketMaster (if available in the area) can boost sales. Paid advertisements in area newspapers and with selected radio stations are also beneficial. The event is promoted as an evening of professional wrestling—live from the community or school auditorium or other suitable site. Providing for autographs and photo sessions with the participants can also pay big dividends in increasing attendance.

Time: It is often necessary to start working on this project some 8 to 9 months (or more) in advance in order to reserve the facility and guarantee the booking of an attractive slate of wrestlers. The sale of tickets should begin at least 5 to 6 weeks prior to the event. The event may run 2 to 3 hours. Reserve 2 to 3 hours to clean up after the event.

Expenditures: The cost of renting the facility can be significant as can the up-front money frequently required to guarantee the appearance of the touring professionals. If there is no cost for the facility, such as a recreation facility or school field house, then the initial expenses can be considerably less. The cost of the professional wrestlers will be paid from the sale of advance tickets. However, the amount of money needed to kick off this fundraiser will be around $500, to be spent on publicity, concessions, and souvenirs.

Personnel (Staff/Volunteers):   This event requires 20 to 30 volunteers and 3 to 7 staff members to market and sell the tickets and to secure sponsors to donate the money for facility rental and for contracting with the professional wrestling organization. These volunteers can also be called upon to staff the concession stand, sell souvenirs, take tickets, and provide for security and supervision. A competent public address announcer is highly recommended.

Risk Management

There are always significant financial risks involved when the success of a fundraiser depends upon ticket sales, especially when the sponsoring group must pay for the cost of the event regardless of ticket sales. Advance ticket sales will provide a clue as to whether there will be adequate attendance. Set a date by which you can cancel the event (due to insufficient ticket sales) without having committed your group to a costly appearance fee. Another way to address this risk is to find an individual or a business to guarantee to cover any financial deficit you may incur. If there is a profit from the event no contribution is needed, but if you incur debt, help is there to bail you out. The sponsor receives publicity, regardless. You can reduce legal liability exposure by insisting that the visiting wrestling organization possess insurance for its own participants and for the audience. If the event is to be held in a school or recreation department facility, consult with the legal counsel of that organization to ensure that there is adequate insurance coverage.

Permits/Licenses

If the event is held at the municipal or city auditorium there probably will be no special permits involved. However, if the site is a school or a recreation facility, check with that organization's attorney to see if a special permit is required (e.g., for concessions or to sell souvenirs). The professional wrestling organization will have the responsibility for securing whatever licenses are needed for the show.

Hints

The professional wrestling group will be able to share a wealth of information about promoting the wrestling evening as well as any special assistance needed. To obtain the names and phone numbers of wrestling organizations, call the sports desk of any major newspaper or contact the facility director of a municipal auditorium or convention center. In some communities where there are large groups of "rabid" wrestling fans this event will be able to generate some big dollars for the recreation or sport group. In other communties, wrestling might not be as popular and the chances for significant profits are greatly diminished. The key is to know the difference and act accordingly.

Selling Athletic Apparel

38

Potential Net Income

$5,000 annually

Complexity/Degree of Difficulty

Moderate

Description

This is an ongoing fundraising project involving the creation of specially designed athletic apparel (such as hats, visors, jackets, sweaters, and shirts) that is sold to fans, parents, and the general public for a profit. The merchandise should be reasonably priced so that the average profit is around $5 per visor or hat, $10 to $15 per shirt, and $25 to $35 per jacket or sweater.

Scheduling

This fundraiser can be initiated at any time of the year. Depending upon the size of the potential market for the items, you can even create a mini-catalog and distribute it via mail or at sport or recreation events.

Resources

Facilities: The items can be sold anywhere, at any indoor or outdoor athletic facility. Unsold inventory should be stored in a convenient but secure location.

Equipment and Supplies: Movable racks and tables are needed so that the merchandise can be displayed and promoted at various events. If necessary, a merchandise catalog and signs can be created. You will also need a cash box with change, order forms, and a notebook to record inventory, sales, expenses, and profits.

Publicity and Promotion: The merchandise can be sold at a host of athletic or recreational events, where point-of-sale signs will attract attention to these items for sale. The items can be promoted by announcements at the school or recreation facility. And, of course, those items sold will themselves serve as promotion for similar items still in inventory.

Time: The selling of specially designed athletic apparel can be an ongoing fundraising effort. Planning can take up to 2 to 3 weeks. It will take 2 to 8 weeks for the wholesalers to fill your order.

Expenditures: Be prepared to spend in the neighborhood of $1,000 for a suitable inventory, display racks, and advertising signs.

Personnel (Staff/Volunteers):   A rotating sales force composed of 10 to 25 volunteers (booster club members or parents) can staff the booths or tables and sell the merchandise at appointed times.

Risk Management

Although the merchandise is purchased wholesale, it is important that your organization not be left with a large amount of unsold merchandise. To prevent this financial disaster, you can obtain samples of the merchandise and take individual, prepaid orders for the items. In this way there is no need for an extensive inventory. However, there can be a significant time gap between when customers place their orders and when they receive the items. If this tactic is not workable, then you must exercise prudent and conservative judgment in ordering an inventory of items from the wholesaler. Seek the advice of the professional wholesaler or manufacturer in terms of style, colors, and sizes. Also, it is imperative that you secure only top-quality merchandise, because each item sold with the name and logo of your organization represents the organization and its programs for as long as the item is used.

Permits/Licenses

Some communities require you to obtain a peddler's permit, hawker's license, or transient business license to sell such merchandise. Check with the town clerk or the office of licenses to see if a permit is required.

Hints

In a junior or senior high school, it may be possible to sell the items in the school bookstore or in the cafeteria before or after school or during study halls. In a recreation department, the items might be placed on sale in the recreation office. If you decide to sell by catalog, customers placing orders should be shown samples of merchandise so they will not be surprised when the order arrives.

Part III

Fundraisers Generating From $5,000 to $10,000

Fundraiser 49.

Halloween Haunted House   *39*

Potential Net Income
$5,500

Complexity/Degree of Difficulty
High

Description
A "haunted house" is created either by making alterations to a vacant building or by erecting a complete, temporary structure containing frightful experiences for youngsters and adults. Profits are generated from the sale of tickets to the haunted house and from the sale of food and drink items.

Scheduling
The haunted house is open for 2 to 3 weeks before Halloween. The site is open each weekday evening from dusk to 10 or 11 p.m. and on weekends from 1 p.m. to 1 a.m.

Resources
Facilities: This fundraiser requires a suitable vacant building or temporary structure that can be easily converted to scare (safely) the living daylights out of those touring the site. Electricity must be available.

Equipment and Supplies: Sound systems (tape recorders will suffice), signs, loudspeakers (for outside of the facility), special decorations, costumes, and lighting are all necessary. Safety equipment such as a first-aid kit, emergency lighting, and fire extinguishers are also required. Signs and banners should be posted outside the building. Tickets will be needed. Also, a cash box with change should be available.

Publicity and Promotion: The publicity consists of advance promotional activities and advertisements, as well as signs and banners outside the building during the time when the haunted house is open. Free mention in the media should easily be obtained due to the nonprofit nature of the fundraiser.

Time: Approximately 2 to 3 months are required to get the building or rooms in shape for the Halloween season. Plan to spend 30 minutes each evening to clean up after guests are gone. Allow an additional week to restore the site to its original condition.

Expenditures: Expenses will center around the costs of equipment, signs and banners, and advertising that cannot be obtained for free; plan on spending $500.

Personnel (Staff/Volunteers):   The project requires 25 to 50 volunteers (among them skilled craftspeople such as carpenters, electricians, and plumbers) to create the haunted house. Some of these volunteers must also staff the site (indoors and outdoors) when it is open to the public and must sell tickets, both on-site and in advance.

Risk Management

An insurance policy covering legal liability exposure should be obtained to cover the owner of the site as well as the sponsoring organization and its members. Safety must be the key word in the entire fundraising effort. Keep in mind that most visitors will be youngsters. Make sure that all walkways are free of obstacles and sharp objects and that all steps are lit. Adults should be available to guide very young children through the maze. Have a well-stocked first-aid kit on hand, and have battery-powered backup lighting installed at key locations inside and outside should the facility experience power failure. The financial risk is limited to the $500 spent creating the haunted house, and that risk is minimized by advance ticket and group sales.

Permits/Licenses

Check with the local building inspector to determine the permits needed for site alterations. Pay special attention to electrical and other safety codes.

Hints

The potential profit depends to a great extent on the amount of expenses you can save by obtaining donated services and goods (such as lumber, nails, and tools). If 3,000 adults and youngsters tour the facility during the 2 to 3 weeks that it is open to the public, there is a possibility of $6,000 in gross profit if the admission charge is only $2 per person. If the charge is $3 per person the gross income climbs to $9,000. This same concept can be put to work with a "Santa Claus Workshop" during the 4 weeks prior to Christmas. In fact, if the haunted house facility or site is not needed for other purposes it could be converted to Santa's workshop in time for the Christmas holidays. Thus, both events could be used to increase the coffers of the recreation or sport organization.

Birthday Cakes for Students   **40**

Potential Net Income

$6,000 annually

Complexity/Degree of Difficulty

Moderate

Description

Three-fourths of the students in a school will have birthdays during the school months of September through June. This fundraiser takes advantage of this fact by allowing parents to order a beautiful birthday cake with candles and individualized decorations and a card to be delivered to their child at school on the youngster's birthday. If the birthday falls on a weekend or holiday, the cake is delivered the preceding school day. The cakes are reasonably priced but provide for a $6 to $7.50 profit for each delivery. If only 400 cakes are ordered throughout the year the sport group can realize a profit of $2,400 to $3,000. If 800 cakes are sold the profit can be $6,000. If this fundraiser is implemented at a college or university, a very high percentage of parents will take part because the students are away from home, often for the first time, and the cake and card become a welcome gift from mom and dad.

Scheduling

A letter and order form are sent to parents just prior to their youngster's birthday. The letter presents several options, each with different costs, to the parents. For example, parents may order a 9-inch cake, a half-sheet cake, cookies, or cup cakes. Each food item is beautifully decorated and is accompanied with an individualized (computerized) birthday card. The cake or cookies can even be delivered with a singing rendition of "Happy Birthday" or another suitable jingle for an additional cost ($1 or $2).

Resources

Facilities: The project requires access to a licensed bakery.

Equipment and Supplies: A computer and laser printer will be of great assistance in generating the personalized letters to the parents and cards to the students. A mailing list will need to be maintained. You will also need a cover letter from the school, postage stamps, and an up-to-date price list.

Publicity and Promotion: Although the initial letter to parents is the primary marketing and promotional tool, don't overlook general advertising in the school's publications. Students can also order cakes or cookies for their friends for any occasion. It is also extremely helpful to provide a cover letter from the school authorities indicating that this is an approved fundraising activity. If no order has been received from the parents within 10 days after the letter is mailed, a volunteer can make a follow-up phone call to the parents. This follow-up from an adult or a student-athlete is frequently a great closing tactic and will result in many additional sales.

Time: This fundraiser can be organized within 5 to 6 days. Letters can be sent to all parents at the start of the school year. Or, a personal letter (created on a computer with a laser printer) can be mailed to a student's parents 30 days prior to the student's birthday. This allows sufficient time for the parents to return their order and for volunteers to create the computerized birthday card, pass on the order to the bakery, and arrange for delivery of the cake and card on the appointed date.

Expenditures: The cost of the birthday cakes, cupcakes, or cookies is the major expenditure of this fundraiser, which should be covered through advance orders. There will be a cost of the postage and the paper from which the personalized letters and birthday cards are created. About $250 seed money to begin the event should suffice.

Personnel (Staff/Volunteers):   You need 10 to 15 volunteers to plan and implement this fundraiser. This includes securing the mailing list, preparing the letters to the parents, relaying the orders for the birthday cakes or cookies to the bakery, creating the birthday cards, and coordinating the pickup from the bakery for same-day delivery to the school.

Risk Management

There is little financial risk since the money is received along with the order; the cake is not ordered from the bakery until the money is in hand. Since the cake is baked and decorated by a professional, licensed bakery the legal liability risk is greatly diminished. Similarly, quality control is maintained as a result of using a professional bakery.

Permits/Licenses

Although no permits or licenses are required in this type of fundraiser, your organization will need to receive permission from the school board or the building principal or from the college administrators to deliver the cakes to students. Usually, high school administrators will establish a specific period (before the first class or during the home room period) when the cakes can be delivered. It will also be necessary to obtain permission to secure a list of students' home addresses and their birthdays from the school.

Hints

In some states it may be permissible for the home economics department to take a role in this fundraising effort by baking the cakes and selling them to the fundraising organization. Or, the home economics department might enter into a partnership with the sport organization in implementing this fundraiser. The challenge in this respect, however, rests in quality control and in terms of legal liability should someone get sick from eating the baked goods. Finally, it might be possible to contract with the school cafeteria to provide the baked goods.

Weekly/Monthly In-House Lottery

41

Potential Net Income

$7,500

Complexity/Degree of Difficulty

Low

Description

Tickets are sold for lottery contests held weekly or monthly by a recreation or athletic organization. Those playing this in-house lottery receive a ticket for each contribution or donation made. Tickets can be sold for $1, $2, or $5. A specified amount of money (depending upon the amount of income anticipated), such as $100 or $200, is given away at each contest. The rest of the money reverts to the coffers of the sponsoring group. The winners of each of the lottery contests can be determined in any number of ways, including using a state's actual winning lottery numbers.

Scheduling

The lottery contests should be scheduled at the same time each week or month so that those interested in playing can anticipate the contest. Tickets can be made available at athletic contests, recreation events, or booster club meetings as well as at specified locations in the community.

Resources

Facilities: The only facility needed is the site for the announcement of lottery winners.

Equipment and Supplies: This project requires lottery tickets, plus supplies for promotion and publicity (i.e., posters, flyers, and displays). If the winners are announced in a group setting, at a game or meeting, you will need to have an adequate microphone and sound system.

Publicity and Promotion: The promotional efforts should emphasize the ease with which it is possible to purchase the lottery tickets. Winners should be publicized in the area media and through flyers, posters, and displays at strategic locations in the school or recreation facility. And, of course, the tangible benefits (profits, and the things these profits will purchase) derived by the recreation or sport organization should be continually publicized. Naturally, most members of the athletic booster club should be interested in participating regularly.

Time: Only 3 to 4 days is required to successfully implement the lottery contest. The key is to hold a lottery regularly throughout the year. Allow 15 minutes for the drawing itself, which can be done in conjunction with another event of the organization.

Expenditures: The cost of the lottery tickets (less than $100) must be paid by the sponsoring group prior to the start of this project. Other expenses are minimal, since winnings are paid out of the gross income generated via ticket sales.

Personnel (Staff/Volunteers):   You will need 10 to 25 volunteers and staff members to sell lottery tickets and promote the entire fundraising effort. Only 1 person is needed to announce the winners.

Risk Management

The sponsoring entity has nothing significant at risk (legally or financially). Perhaps, in some communities, the fact that the fundraising effort hinges on a game of chance might be looked upon with some skepticism if not outright disapproval. However, the lottery, if legal in your state and if handled well, can be a most effective fundraiser.

Permits/Licenses

Investigate local ordinances (town clerk) and the state law (State Gaming Board or other similar office) in respect to securing the necessary permits.

Hints

This type of fundraising effort can become a permanent fixture in your arsenal. Human nature being what it is, people enjoy games of chance. The fact that these games of chance support the athletic or recreation program makes the weekly or monthly in-house lottery that much more attractive.

5-Kilometer Race

42

Potential Net Income

$8,000

Complexity/Degree of Difficulty

Moderate

Description

A 5-kilometer race is planned through a scenic area of the community. Any number of runners can be accommodated, as many as 2,000 to 5,000 men and women of all ages or as few as 100 to 200. Profits are derived from entrance fees, which may be $10 or more. Or, runners can solicit pledges from individuals and businesses based on the number of kilometers the runners actually complete. For example, a runner might solicit 50 pledges of $1 per kilometer; if the runner completes all 5 kilometers she or he will raise $250. Participants from all segments of the public can be attracted to this event.

Scheduling

The race should be scheduled on a weekend, perhaps one of the weekends associated with physical fitness or health such as the National Physical Fitness Week, usually held in early May. Also, the event should be scheduled when the weather is most likely to cooperate, although the race can be held even if it rains.

Resources

Facilities: The event requires a temporarily designated 5-kilometer course. The course can consist of streets, sidewalks, cross-country paths, or some combination of these.

Equipment and Supplies: Flyers and posters will be needed to publicize the event. Runners will need tags and pins. You will need to print registration forms, release forms, and pledge sheets. You will also need a notebook or binder to keep track of these forms and pledges. On the day of the race you will need a cash box with change and digital stop watches. Prizes and awards for the runners should be donated by area businesses and individuals. Also, you will need signs, refreshment tents and first-aid stations, trash cans, extra tents, and maps. Walkie-talkies are a big boon to communication among volunteers and staff.

Publicity and Promotion: Publicity should be initiated at least 4 weeks before the race through free mention in the media, distribution of flyers, and display of posters. Solicit runners by contacting service organizations, schools, clubs, and businesses. Of course those associated with the sponsoring organization as well as athletes, parents of athletes, booster club members, and fans are all prime candidates to participate. Awards (medals, ribbons, and T-shirts) may be given to all participants who complete the course. Special prizes are given to the first-, second-, and third-place runners in different categories according to their age and sex. Additional support for this event can be solicited from area hospitals, physicians, and sports medicine clinics and from the American Red Cross and the local Heart Association. If business or corporate sponsorships are solicited (thereby generating more funds), signs designating these sponsors can be made and displayed along the course.

Time: Planning time can consume upward of several months, while the race itself can be completed in less than 2 hours. Allow 2 to 3 weeks to collect pledges. Schedule 2 to 3 hours after the event to clean up the staging area (where the race is started), the rest areas, and the area surrounding the finish line.

Expenditures: Expenditures will be necessary for publicity and promotion as well as for the awards and prizes that are not donated. Plan to spend up to $300 in seed money.

Personnel (Staff/Volunteers):   About 15 to 25 volunteers and staff members are needed not only to help promote and publicize the race but also to solicit financial support from area businesses. Volunteers are needed to help staff the start and finish areas of the race (keeping times and records) and to be at various checkpoints along the course providing refreshments, directions, first aid, encouragement, and security.

Risk Management

For liability protection you must provide one or more first-aid stations along the race course. A standard release form should be signed by each participant (parental signature required if participant is under 18 years of age) stating that the individual is in good health and is aware of the risks involved in this event. This release document should hold harmless the organizers and those working the event from responsibility for accidents and injuries other than for gross negligence. Additionally, you might want to require that runners provide written evidence of physical fitness (a physician's statement). The financial risk associated with this fundraising project is moderate because the income generated from the event should cover necessary expenditures.

Permits/Licenses

If the race course covers private property, permission must be obtained from the owner for the use of the path or course. Permission from the local authorities must be obtained if the community roads are to be used by the runners. Having the streets blocked off for the safety of the runners requires cooperation with community law enforcement and municipal administration officials.

Hints

This race could also be planned as a 10-kilometer event, although this would significantly increase the amount of time the race takes. A sufficient number of race coordinators must be stationed strategically along the way to provide assistance and directions to the runners. Naturally, this type of event can easily become an annual event, providing significant money for your organization.

Hoop-a-Thon

43

Potential Net Income
$8,500

Complexity/Degree of Difficulty
Moderate

Description
This fundraising project involves the solicitation of pledges from individuals in the community based upon the number of baskets made during a 6-hour basketball marathon. The event is organized with various three-player teams continually rotating to compete with one another. When a team reaches 20 baskets it rotates to another basket to play another team. Since not all teams will conclude at the same time there will be times when a team must wait until an opposing team is available. Each team must have at least a 3-minute break before beginning a new game against new opponents. Additionally, each hour all teams take a 5-minute break. Other than these periodic breaks all the teams play continuously throughout the hoop-a-thon.

At the end of the 6 hours the team with the most baskets scored is declared the overall winner; its members, as well as members of the second-, third-, and fourth-place teams, receive special prizes and awards donated by area businesses. Individual awards are also given in recognition of outstanding athletic performance and outstanding solicitation of pledges. All participants receive tournament T-shirts and hats.

A typical hoop-a-thon might involve 48 adults and youngsters participating on 16 teams and playing on 8 courts. On an average, individual teams will take approximately 15 minutes to score 15 baskets. Thus in a 6-hour period a team can conceivably score 360 baskets. Donors pledging 10¢ per basket scored by a specific team will be committing themselves to a maximum of $36 for the entire hoop-a-thon. And, if each of the 48 participants has commitments from just five different individuals, the total gross contribution for the 240 contributors will be in the neighborhood of $8,640. If 10 people make such pledges for each participant the gross profits will be over $16,000.

Scheduling
The hoop-a-thon can be scheduled during the afternoon or evening, Friday through Sunday.

Resources

Facilities: The optimal facility is an indoor gymnasium with numerous baskets so that at least 6 to 10 three-on-three half-court games can be played simultaneously. An outdoor playing area with sufficient baskets and playing space will suffice, although the weather can play havoc with an outdoor event.

Equipment and Supplies: In addition to items such as basketballs, scoreboards, and stat books, refreshments and a first-aid station for the athletes are necessary. You need to obtain awards, prizes, and souvenirs (T-shirts and hats) either as donations or at reduced cost. Pledge sheets need to be given to all participants.

Publicity and Promotion: Advance publicity through the media is most helpful, but the key to the success of this fundraiser is the solicitation of pledges. The importance of person-to-person sales cannot be overemphasized.

Time: Planning this event will take 1 to 2 weeks. Solicitation of pledges and donations will take 3 to 4 weeks. Plan on spending 1 or 2 hours setting up. The hoop-a-thon competition will last 6 hours. You need to allow 2 to 3 hours for cleaning up the facility.

Expenditures: Few expenditures are needed since the site for the games as well as the equipment and supplies will be sought as donations. You will need $50 to initiate the project.

Personnel (Staff/Volunteers):   You will need 10 to 12 volunteers to staff and manage the hoop-a-thon and to solicit donated equipment and supplies. Additionally, 1 or 2 staff members should coordinate overall planning and implementation.

Risk Management

It is suggested that the donors be assured that their donations will not exceed a specific dollar amount. For example, a prospective donor might make a 10¢ per basket pledge with a maximum obligation of $40. In this way, there will be no surprises and no ill will created if a team actually scores 500 baskets. There is no financial risk involved in this event. However, there is always liability exposure during athletic activities in terms of participants' being injured. This is especially important for a marathon-type event. The participant is often asked to provide a statement from a physician or nurse (and one from a parent if the participant is a minor) stating that the individual is in good health and able to participate in the hoop-a-thon. Also, the participant must sign an agreement releasing the organizers and those working the event from responsibility for accidents and injuries except for gross negligence.

Permits/Licenses

None are needed.

Hints

This fundraiser could easily become an annual event. You might think about charging an admission fee for spectators; corporate sponsorships and donations can also significantly increase profits.

Overnight Youth Sport Summer Camp

44

Potential Net Income

$8,800

Complexity/Degree of Difficulty

High

Description

This fundraiser centers around a 5-day, overnight, youth sport camp for basketball, volleyball, soccer, baseball, softball, or other sport. Youngsters in 5th grade through high school are eligible to attend; tuition is around $220. Additional profit centers include concessions as well as sales of sourvenir merchandise. The camp either can involve both boys and girls or can be organized as a single-sex camp.

Scheduling

The camp is scheduled from Sunday afternoon through Friday afternoon. It is an overnight affair with the athletes staying Sunday through Thursday nights in dormitories. Daily activities begin at 7 a.m. with breakfast, and lights-out is at 10:30 p.m. There should be extensive activities scheduled from dawn to dusk each day. In addition to targeting specific sport activities, you should allocate time for general recreation, for example, in the swimming pool.

Resources

Facilities: A facility that includes sufficient indoor and outdoor space to accommodate the number of youngsters is required; a college is an ideal setting. Naturally, adequate dormitory space and a professionally staffed cafeteria are prerequisites.

Equipment and Supplies: Promotional flyers/registration forms need to be mailed prior to the event. Balls and other necessary sport paraphernalia are required. Additionally, T-shirts, jerseys, athletic training/sports medicine supplies, and concession and merchandise items are also necessary. Most of these items can be obtained free or at reduced cost. Arrangements for meals must be made, and an evaluation form created.

Publicity and Promotion: Promotional flyers and registration forms need to be sent to schools, athletic teams, and coaches throughout the geographic target area, which could extend 200 to 300 miles (within a day's driving distance). Advertisements can be included in state or national athletic publications. Additional publicity can be generated through public address announcements at athletic contests in area schools.

Time: From December through April, time is spent confirming the availability of the facilities, implementing extensive advertising activities, and lining up the necessary staff. The camp is held during the summer months for a week, Sunday afternoon through Friday afternoon.

Expenditures: A professionally designed flyer, which includes an application or a registration form, can cost between $250 and $500 (including postage). It is advisable to secure a well-known coach to spend a morning or afternoon at the camp for a cost of around $500 to $1,500. This headliner serves as a main attraction for the young campers. Other coaches are hired for $100 to $150 per week, plus room and board. The total cost of the staff, facility use, food, and dormitory accommodations generally should not exceed 60% of the gross income. Thus, if 100 athletes attend the camp at $220 each there will be approximately $22,000 gross profit (or more) and a net profit of around $8,800. Of course, if the costs of the facilities and staff are reduced the net profit will be correspondingly greater. T-shirts, hats, and other souvenirs can be ordered once the advance reservations are received. Seed money for the camp promotion will be in the neighborhood of $500.

Personnel (Staff/Volunteers):   The professional camp staff consists of area high school and college coaches with perhaps one big-name coach. If college eligibility rules permit, additional coaching and teaching assistance can be provided by area college athletes. There should be a professional staff member for every 8 to 10 campers. A certified NATA trainer should also be on hand throughout the week. The coaching staff can double as dormitory counselors by supervising campers in the dorms at night. The project may require a total of 20 to 35 staff, depending upon the number of campers.

Risk Management

Campers must provide signed affidavits from their parents or guardians stating that the youngsters are covered under the family's insurance policy and that they have permission to attend the camp. Be sure to inform the local hospital when the camp will be held so its staff will be alerted for possible admits. The presence of a qualified athletic trainer (NATA certified) on site also helps reduce the legal liability exposure of camp staff. On the last day of camp, a staff member should examine each camper's room to determine whether there is any damage for which the camper is liable. Before parents depart the camp site on Friday afternoon, they must pay for any damage or outstanding obligations. If this message is conveyed to parents and campers during the Sunday afternoon orientation, the likelihood of theft or damage to the dorm rooms is significantly curtailed.

Permits/Licenses

In many states it is necessary to satisfy one or more state or county laws regarding the establishment of sport schools or recreation camps. Additionally, you need to carefully review the state high school athletic association rules so as not to run afoul of any eligibility regulation. Permits for concessions must be secured as required.

Hints

Each camper receives a complimentary camp T-shirt. Additional shirts may be purchased, as may other souvenirs. These items are great advertisement for subsequent camps. Also, each camper receives an individual evaluation sheet that outlines his or her strengths and weaknesses. This is a great public relations tool and also a real help for the individual camper. To ensure a sufficient number of campers, especially in the initial year of the camp, it is sometimes helpful to give tuition discounts to campers from schools that have five or more athletes at camp. Also, coaches who are on staff tend to encourage athletes from their schools to attend. In some states it is illegal, according to the various high school eligibility rules, for a high school coach to teach or coach one of his or her own athletes at a summer camp; keep this in mind when assigning coaches to work with youngsters. Securing a business sponsor to help underwrite some of the costs (T-shirts, souvenirs, balls, etc.) will help ensure that the camp is a money-maker. Once a camp has been successful, its continued existence is made much easier by positive public relations and word-of-mouth advertisement by athletes and parents.

Cow Drop

45

Potential Net Income

$9,000

Complexity/Degree of Difficulty

Moderate

Description

Any large area, such as a football, soccer, or softball field, is marked off with field-marking paint into 3-foot-square parcels. On a field 198 feet long and 60 feet wide there can be 1,235 squares. Tickets representing "ownership" for each of the squares are sold on a blind basis, that is, buyers don't know the exact location of their squares until they have purchased the tickets. On the day of the event a cow is let loose on the field. The winner of the grand prize is identified when the cow makes its "dropping" on a specific square on the field (the winner's ticket number corresponds with the square number). The prize may be either a cash prize or a product (the value of which is predetermined by the amount of the tickets to be sold). If 1,200 tickets are sold for $10 each, the gross income is $12,000. If the grand prize is $2,500 the income for your group is $9,500, before payment of any other expenses.

Scheduling

It is preferable to schedule the event on a Saturday or Sunday afternoon during favorable weather. Since the actual time it takes for the cow to make its "drop" varies from just a few moments to several hours, it is recommended that other promotional activities be scheduled in conjunction with the "Cow Drop." For example, picnics and outdoor competitive or recreational games can be scheduled on an adjacent field while the crowd waits for the cow to do its duty.

Resources

Facilities: Permission to use a sufficiently large field, preferably fenced, must be obtained well in advance of any preliminary advertisement. (See "Description" for an explanation of how to mark the field.)

Equipment and Supplies: A rented or borrowed cow and a means of transporting it are essential for this event. Field-marking paint and a paint machine are also necessary. A microphone and loudspeaker system and an exciting announcer will enhance enthusiasm as the crowd is kept aware of the cow's meandering. A map identifying the location of squares on the field can be placed on a portable bulletin board at the field (this may also generate publicity for the event). Smaller versions of the map may be distributed to those attending the event. You will also need numbered tickets and promotional flyers and posters.

Publicity and Promotion: Advance media and person-to-person publicity should precede ticket sales. Distribute flyers and posters throughout the community, targeting especially the local businesses. Public address announcements made at other athletic and recreational events will help hype this unique event.

Time: Planning this event can take 1 to 2 weeks. The selling window should be limited to no more than 3 weeks. Setup time, including marking the field, can be 4 to 6 hours. The event can take place in a few hours. Cleaning up can be done in an hour or less.

Expenditures: Expenditures are limited to the cost of publicity (printed materials and other forms of advertisements) and paint; the rental costs of the land, the cow, and the paint machine; and the money or prizes to be given to the winner. Of course if these items and services are donated, so much the better. Generally, the event can be implemented with less than $300.

Personnel (Staff/Volunteers):   You will have to rely heavily on volunteers, about 30. The event requires an announcer, judges, cow handlers, a driver of the truck for the animal, on-site supervisors, and crowd control personnel as well as those involved in publicity and ticket sales.

Risk Management

Potential danger areas include the handling of the animal on its way to and from the event and when it is released onto the field. An experienced handler should attend to the cow as it meanders throughout the field. Check with an attorney and with a competent insurer to determine how to limit and protect against legal liability exposure. The financial risks involved in this fundraiser are minimal and are essentially limited to costs already outlined plus insurance coverage, if necessary.

Permits/Licenses

Check with the town clerk or licensing bureau to determine if a specific permit is needed in your community. Also, some organizers have contacted the local National Society for the Prevention of Cruelty to Animals

(NSPCA) to request that a representative be on hand to forestall any criticism.

Hints

A panel of judges will determine the owner of the square on which the cow makes its drop. Their decision shall be final. Prior to the event the cow should be amply fed and watered by its owner. Plan for and advertise the fact the if the cow does not make its drop within a specific time frame, perhaps 2 to 3 hours, you will use the ticket stubs to conduct a drawing for the prize. Or, the 3-foot-square site on which the cow is standing at a specified time can be declared the winning parcel. In this way the event will close within a reasonable period of time.

50-50 Drawing

46

Potential Net Income

$10,000 annually

Complexity/Degree of Difficulty

Low

Description

Tickets are sold for a drawing to be held during halftime of an athletic contest or at a designated time during a recreational event. One half of the money from ticket sales will be given to the lucky winner, with the remaining half going to the fundraising group. Tickets can be sold for $1 or more. Thus, if 600 people buy tickets at $1, the sponsoring organization will realize a net profit of $300 per event.

Scheduling

Schools and athletic organizations can sell tickets at their sporting events, while recreational organizations can sell tickets at any of their special events. *The key to big profits is to make this an anticipated event at all contests or events*. Thus an organization with 35 home contests or special events in a year can net some $300 per event, for a grand total of $10,500.

Resources

Facilities: No special facilities are needed because the drawings are piggybacked upon regularly scheduled events.

Equipment and Supplies: This project requires a roll of double tickets, a bowl out of which to pull the winning ticket, and the use of a microphone and speaker system to announce the winner. Double tickets are two tickets attached to each other having the same serial or identification number. When the tickets are sold the purchaser retains one ticket and the duplicate ticket is placed in the bowl. Tables strategically positioned near the entrance to the event as well as adjacent to the concession stand can greatly enhance sales. Ticket sellers will need pouches to hold money from the sales of tickets. Signs can be made to advertise the event.

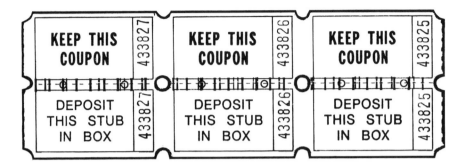

Publicity and Promotion: High visibility at the event where the drawing will be held is required, as is publicity preceding the event itself. Everyone attending the event should be made aware of the drawing and how the profits will be used. One way to accomplish this is to offer the tickets for sale near the event ticket booths and at the facility entrance. Additionally, ticket sellers can walk throughout the facility during the early part of the athletic event, offering spectators the opportunity to buy tickets. Periodically during the event and just before the drawing is held the PA announcer can share the total amount of the pot, thus encouraging last-minute purchases. Make the actual drawing of the winning ticket and the presentation of the money a big deal at halftime or other convenient breakpoints (such as intermission) so as to increase the exposure and excitement of the drawing.

Time: This project can be planned and volunteers solicited in as little as 1 or 2 days. Typically, tickets are sold only on the day of the contest or event, just prior to and during the actual event. However, advance tickets can be sold as well.

Expenditures: There are minimal expenses for the drawing. The roll of tickets and the poster boards necessary to make signs will cost less than $100 for the year. Half of the money raised will be given as prize money to the winner of each drawing.

Personnel (Staff/Volunteers):   About 5 volunteers are needed to sell the tickets at most games, but more may be needed at larger events. For the whole year, you will need a core of 25 to 30 dedicated volunteers to sell tickets. A responsible adult should draw the winning ticket and award the cash prize amid much fanfare.

Risk Management

This fundraiser involves no financial risk since the profit comes from ticket sales. There is also little liability risk inherent in this fundraiser.

Permits/Licenses

Some locales may require a permit for this game of chance. Contact your town clerk or municipal offices to determine whether a permit or license is necessary.

Hints

To establish a perception of fairness and honesty, only adult staff or volunteers should draw for the winning ticket. Strict accounting procedures should be in place in terms of recording the number of tickets sold and the amount of money received. You can structure the contest so that when the pot reaches $1,000 or more, the prize is divided between two winners or more. Or, there could remain one big winner who takes home 50% of whatever amount is generated through the ticket sales. Frequently people who would not normally buy a ticket will purchase one or two when the pot reaches a rather high amount, that is, several thousand dollars.

Selling Products From National Fundraising Companies

47

Potential Net Income

$10,000

Complexity/Degree of Difficulty

Moderate

Description

Patterned after the famous Girl Scout cookie campaigns, this project can be successfully implemented by any group that has a significant number of participants. There are numerous national and regional wholesalers that fill orders for a variety of items—both edible and nonedible—sold by fundraising groups. These groups sell the merchandise (frequently using a catalog) to the general public for a substantial profit, sometimes as much as 60%. This project is not a so-called candy bar sale in which the school must *buy* candy and then resell it.

Scheduling

This fundraiser can be conducted at any time of the year. However, a selling campaign planned around holidays such as Christmas, Thanksgiving, Halloween, Valentine's Day, Mother's Day, or Easter, and involving merchandise related to one of these holidays, is especially effective.

Resources

Facilities: The only facility needed is a site where the merchandise will be received from the wholesaler and stored for a very short time until individual sellers deliver it to the purchasers.

Equipment and Supplies: Everything is provided by the wholesaler, including four-color catalogs and order forms.

Publicity and Promotion: The program can be successful even with minimal advance publicity. The key in promoting this type of sales campaign is to quickly acquaint potential buyers with the purpose of the sale and with the value of the merchandise. Showing potential customers the beautiful four-color catalogs and explaining how the proceeds will benefit the nonprofit athletic or recreation organization are big selling and promotional points.

Time: Planning this event, selecting a suitable wholesaler, and organizing volunteers can take 1 to 2 weeks. The actual selling of the items should be limited to no more than 7 to 14 days. A longer selling window is not necessary and can, in fact, hinder the selling process. A 1-hour afternoon training session will help educate the youngsters in terms of appropriate sales tactics and will provide them with fundamental awareness of safety concerns. Once ordered, presold merchandise can be shipped and on-site within 7 to 10 days; the merchandise can then be delivered to customers over a weekend.

Expenditures: Typically, the wholesaler is paid after the money is collected from purchasers. Thus, no up-front money is needed. Catalogs and order blanks are provided free from the company.

Personnel (Staff/Volunteers):   Usually those youngsters involved in the recreational or sport program will be the sales force, with adult supervision and guidance. Some programs involve as many as 200 to 300 volunteers, while others can have a successful program with as few as 30 to 50 helpers. Parents can also become expert sellers of the items (especially candy products) by taking catalogs to work, passing them around the office or factory, and signing up purchasers.

Risk Management

In terms of liability risks, there is always potential for accidents when youngsters sell door-to-door. Appropriate adult supervision must be provided. Holding training sessions for youngsters in which both safety matters and appropriate selling tactics are dealt with is highly recommended. There is minimal financial risk since all costs are paid from the profit from sales. One responsible adult (staff or volunteer) should have responsibility for record keeping, ordering, and handling the monies.

Permits/Licenses

Peddler's permits may be required in some communities if the youngsters sell door-to-door. Check with the local licensing bureau (town clerk or municipal offices).

Hints

There are actually two types of selling programs. First, there is the "take-order" program, when sales of specific items are made from catalogs. Within a few days after the end of the selling period all the merchandise sold by the group is shipped to a central location. The youngsters who sold the items then deliver them and collect the money. In this type of a program the variety of items sold can be rather extensive. The second variation is called the "point-of-sale" campaign. In this situation the youngsters actually carry a limited amount of merchandise, which they can sell on the spot. Both of these programs can be equally productive. The advantage with the take-order program is that a wider range of merchandise can be marketed. However, this program requires a second trip to the customer to deliver the merchandise and to collect the money. The prime advantage of the point-of-sale campaign is that cash is obtained and the merchandise is given to the customer when the sale is made. You obtain names and addresses of national and regional companies by checking the yellow pages in any large city.

Phone-a-Thon

48

Potential Net Income

$10,000

Complexity/Degree of Difficulty

Moderate

Description

Volunteers, seeking contributions for the various programs sponsored by the sport or recreation organization, make phone calls to targeted individuals and businesses. Organizers subsequently mail out solicitation forms to those who have pledged contributions.

Scheduling

A phone-a-thon can be scheduled for a single day or for any number of days during a 2-week period. The sessions should be held on weekday evenings (when individuals are targeted for solicitation) and in the mornings (when businesses are called).

Resources

Facilities: This requires a room or a number of adjacent rooms where a number of telephones may be used simultaneously.

Equipment and Supplies: A typed script for the callers to follow in their sales pitch to the potential donors is a great asset. The callers will also need a pledge sheet on which to record the amount of pledges made and the reasons why an individual is not able to contribute at this time. Letters and fact sheets (mailed prior to the event to explain the phone-a-thon) are helpful. A computer, appropriate software, a letter-quality printer, stationery, and postage must be secured, as well as a list of names, addresses, and phone numbers for prospective donors. Refreshments for those volunteers making the phone calls are also necessary.

Publicity and Promotion: Letters that have been personally signed and addressed, and mailed about 10 days prior to the phone-a-thon to those who will be called, are helpful in alerting the prospective donors to the purpose of the call and in reminding them of the need for financial support. A carefully prepared fact sheet accompanying the letter can help sell the need for support in a professional manner.

Time: Planning this fundraiser, which includes soliciting and training volunteers and compiling a list of prospective donors, can take 2 to 3 weeks. The evening phone-a-thon sessions should be scheduled from 7 until 9:30 p.m., while the morning sessions should be planned for between 8:30 a.m. and noon. You may need to spend an hour cleaning up after each session.

Expenditures: Expenditures include the costs of the mailing to the prospective donors plus refreshments for those staffing the phone lines ($150). The use of a computer, printer, and office space can be donated.

Personnel (Staff/Volunteers): You will need 10 to 20 volunteers (youngsters and adults) to staff the phones during each phone-a-thon session. Youngsters as young as 13 or 14 years of age can take part in the phone-a-thon as long as they feel comfortable in making the calls and have adequate phone skills. If the phone-a-thon is to take place over more than a single day it may require as many as 30 to 45 volunteers, since not all will want to work every session.

Risk Management

The greatest risk is turning people off and creating negative public relations through improper phone etiquette or poor solicitation skills. Thus, if you are using young or inexperienced phone solicitors it is imperative that you conduct a training session (or more than one) and provide an adult monitor in the phone area during sessions to answer any questions and to provide assistance and counseling when needed. The key is that no hard selling shall take place and thus no ill feelings will be generated. There is no legal liability exposure or significant financial risk in this fundraiser.

Permits/Licenses

None are needed.

Hints

Phone solicitors should mention a range of cash contributions (for example, $100 to $250, or $50 to $100) when speaking to a prospective contributor. If the person is not able to donate at the level mentioned, the solicitor should reduce the range and ask if the person would feel comfortable contributing at that level. The objective is for the phone solicitor to get the prospect to donate some amount, even if it is merely $5. In determining which names (and phone numbers) shall make up the prospect list, start with those who have contributed (in any way) to the program in the past. Others to be targeted as prime prospects are parents whose youngsters are presently involved or have been involved in the program or similar programs, as well as individuals who have previously supported youth or sports activities and recreation programs. The point is that the phone calls are made to individuals and businesses targeted because of a specific factor that leads you to believe that they will contribute. A variation of the phone-a-thon involves adult volunteers calling from their own homes at their convenience during the 2-week solicitation window.

Golf Tournament

49

Potential Net Income

$10,000

Complexity/Degree of Difficulty

High

Description

A golf tournament for men and women is held at a local country club in conjunction with a buffet dinner in the early evening. Tickets are sold for $100 to $125 (or what is feasible in your area), which includes the cost of golfing, a cart for each foursome, and the dinner. With 100 golfers anticipated, the income from advance ticket sales is between $10,000 and $12,500. Signs, to be placed at each green and each tee, are sold for $100 each to area businesses and individuals who place their logos or individualized messages on them. Thus, the 36 signs generate another $3,600 in income for a total of $13,600 before expenses are deducted. If 150 golfers take part, the total gross income can range from $18,600 to $22,350.

Scheduling

This golf tournament can be scheduled on a Saturday or Sunday in the spring, summer, or fall. The golfing can take place from 9 a.m. to approximately 5 or 6 p.m. Volunteers or staff members in a golf cart travel around the course throughout the day handing out free sodas, hot dogs, and snacks to the golfers and generally monitoring and directing play. Around 6 or 6:30 p.m., a happy hour is held, followed by dinner at 7 p.m. During or immediately following the dinner, a master of ceremony distributes awards to individual and group winners of various contests held during the tournament (for example, low gross, closest to the pin, or longest drive).

Resources

Facilities: It is necessary to secure use of an 18-hole golf course for an entire day. Also needed is an on-site banquet area that can serve an adequate meal for a reasonable cost.

Equipment and Supplies: The event requires advance tickets, golf carts, score sheets, and various prizes and trophies. Naturally, the pro shop is open to meet the needs of the golfers. Advertisement signs will need to be created for each hole. The clubhouse should have a sound system and bar equipment. You will also need snack foods and refreshments.

Publicity and Promotion: Advance tickets are sold through formal advertising efforts, by placing tickets on sale at area businesses, and, of course, by individual supporters and boosters selling tickets to their friends, co-workers, and acquaintances. You should be able to obtain extensive free publicity due to the nonprofit nature of the organization and the purpose for which the tournament is being held. The "window" for advance publicity and ticket selling can range from 3 to 5 weeks.

Time: Planning for the initial golf tournament can take up to 3 or 4 months. Subsequent tournaments will require less advance planning time since you will have learned from the experience. The dinner and awards ceremony should not last more than 2 hours. Setting up may take 2 to 3 hours, and cleaning up less than 2.

Expenditures: Attempt to reduce all expenses by soliciting trade-outs or securing the use of the site, carts, signs, awards, and even the banquet food for reduced prices, if not for free. Rent for the golf carts can usually be reduced to $5 to $10 per person. An excellent meal, happy hour, and the roving golf cart with refreshments might run around $18 to $25 per person. Add to this the cost of the 18 holes of golf (at a reduced cost of $20 per person), and the total expenses run to approximately $43 to $55 per person. In this scenario you would have approximately $45 to $57 net profit for each golfer if the cost of the golf tourney is $100. If the cost is $125 the net profit can range between $70 and $82 per person. Naturally, any time costs are reduced the profits jump. Seed money to kick off this event will be around $250.

Personnel (Staff/Volunteers):   The event requires 35 to 50 volunteers plus 1 or 2 staff members, who need to be coordinated in selling the tickets, establishing golfing rules and policies, planning the meal, keeping tabs on golfers' scores, and contracting for the golf course. Having golf experts plan and coordinate the golfing aspect of this event (including individual contests for men and women) will go a long way toward making this fundraiser truly enjoyable and successful.

Risk Management

The weather is frequently the greatest risk factor for the golf tournament. Nothing dampens golfers' enthusiasm more than pouring rain. However, with advance ticket sales the financial risk is significantly minimized. Unless the owner of the golf course closes it, the tournament should be held regardless of the weather. If the course is closed, the happy hour and dinner should still be held, but no refunds for the tournament should be given. Because most courses have their calendars full for weeks, if not months, in the future, a rain date is not a good idea. The second risk centers around the ability of staff and volunteers to sell a sufficient number of tickets. Securing a sponsor to underwrite a potential shortfall of ticket sales is a way to help cushion the financial blow should insufficient tickets be sold to cover expenses. The legal exposure in terms of liability is usually covered by the golf course's blanket insurance policy.

Permits/Licenses

None are needed. The golf course food service management will take care of all licences for the distribution of food and alcohol.

Hints

It is advisable to reserve a site early; in many communities access to a golf course is severely limited in good weather. Also, a shortage of courses in some locales causes many operators to be reluctant to give prime starting times to an outside group or even to reserve a significant portion of the course to such a group unless a large number of foursomes can be guaranteed or the owner of the course has a special affiliation with the sponsoring group. The best course of action is to solicit the assistance of site owners who are receptive to the purpose of your group and will give you a good deal on an all-day package including golf carts, awards, and dinner.

Mile of Art Show

50

Potential Net Income

$10,000

Complexity/Degree of Difficulty

High

Description

Works by artists and craftspeople, involving all types of media, are displayed for sale on tables or in booths along a winding sidewalk or outdoor path. Admission to the "Mile of Art Show" is free to the public. Profits are made from rentals ($50 to $75) of 8-foot by 12-foot spaces for the display of the artists' work. Additional profits can be generated through the sale of concession items and souvenirs. In addition to paying a fee to exhibit, each artist agrees to donate a piece of work, all of which are then auctioned during the 2 days of the art show, with the proceeds going to the sponsoring group.

Scheduling

The event should be scheduled during the spring, summer, or fall, when the weather is nice. The better the weather the greater the likelihood of a successful fundraising project.

Resources

Facilities: An outdoor path or sidewalk that extends for a quarter or half mile or so is needed. Restroom facilities should be available. Adequate space for parking must be available.

Equipment and Supplies: Invitations and registration forms will need to be sent to area artists. You will need stationery and postage as well as materials for publicity. Tables and chairs should be provided for each art exhibitor although many artists will provide their own display tables and racks. Concession stand equipment and supplies are needed if your group intends to sell food and drink. It is suggested that you establish numerous concession sites along the walk area to take advantage of the crowd, so you will also need plenty of trash cans. A first-aid station should also be established.

Publicity and Promotion: Extensive promotion and publicity are needed to attract top-notch artists and exhibitors. Obtaining names and addresses from local and statewide art groups and craft groups and then mailing invitations (with registration forms) to individual artists and artisans will result in a large number of participants. And, naturally, advertisements within the various media are essential to inform the general public about the free opportunity to view outstanding art and purchase items at reasonable prices. You can obtain much free advertising through notices in the art sections of area newpapers.

Time: Two to three months are normally required to plan and organize the event. The art show is usually scheduled for Friday afternoon and evening, all day Saturday, and Sunday afternoon. Allow 3 to 4 hours for artists to set up their booths, and plan for at least that much time for cleaning up afterwards.

Expenditures: Expenditures include the costs of publicity and promotion, postage, and printed materials. You also must rent the tables and chairs, if they are not otherwise available. Expenses can be as high as $500.

Personnel (Staff/Volunteers): This event requires an extensive network of volunteers, 30 to 45, supported by 3 to 5 professional staff members of the sponsoring organization. These individuals will solicit noteworthy exhibitors and spread the news throughout the community about the

"Mile of Art Show." Volunteers will also be needed to assist in parking the guests' vehicles.

Risk Management

The greatest risk is that the event will not attract sufficient exhibitors of substantial quality and reputation during its initial year. The quality and quantity of the exhibitors will determine attendance at the event. Hence, effective publicity is essential. In terms of legal liability, be sure that the site owner's insurance policy provides adequate coverage in light of the large number of visitors walking around the sidewalks and footpaths and using the parking lot. Provide adult supervision to ensure that there are no parking problems. The financial risk can be sizable depending upon the costs incurred in advertising and in soliciting quality exhibitors. Financial risk is minimized when materials are donated (postage, stationery, concessions) and by using free publicity (public announcements in the media).

Permits/Licenses

If the event is held on your organization's own site there are usually no permits required; however, you should double-check with the municipal offices of your community. Concession permits may need to be secured. Also, it would be wise to notify the local police so the officers can plan for traffic control.

Hints

When soliciting exhibitors, emphasize how the sponsoring group will promote and publicize the show. When well-known artists have agreed to attend, highlight their names to attract other exhibitors and publicity for the event. After the "Mile of Art Show" has been successful for a number of years, it may be necessary to accept exhibitors only on a juried basis. This event is a natural for an annual fundraising project and can result in significant profits and excellent public relations. There are two courses of action in the event of inclement weather. Either move all of the exhibits inside a facility that is large enough, or provide each booth or table with a plastic covering or other similar protection. Many experienced exhibitors will bring suitable tarpaulins in case of inclement weather.

Annual Fall Bazaar

51

Potential Net Income

$10,000

Complexity/Degree of Difficulty

High

Description

This outdoor bazaar features a wide variety of ethnic foods and beverages for sale as well as musical entertainment representing different cultures. In addition, a wide range of merchandise, including sourvenirs, toys, clothes, and crafts, is available for purchase. Those in attendance are also free to browse. Income is generated from general admission ticket sales and the renting of 10-foot by 15-foot spaces for those selling food and merchandise.

Scheduling

This event is scheduled for the early fall, taking advantage of the usually excellent and mild weather. Its length can vary.

Resources

Facilities: The event requires an outdoor area large enough to accommodate 1,000 to 5,000 people, plus adequate parking facilities. The site must be large enough that the different groups playing music will not drown one another out. Outdoor fields adjacent to hardtop parking surfaces can be ideal.

Equipment and Supplies: Tickets will need to be printed, and you will need materials for making signs and flyers. Require food vendors to have their own cooking equipment and supplies. You should provide an ample number of tables and chairs that people can use as they partake of the food and listen to the music, and have available plenty of trash receptacles. Tents or individual booths can be erected to suit the needs of the exhibitors, or vendors can be expected to bring their own portable booths or tents and cash boxes. Access to electricity is imperative, as is rental of portable toilets. You will need to set up a first-aid station. As the bazaar grows in popularity year after year, you might need to construct portable, wooden structures to house the various vendors.

Publicity and Promotion: Advance ticket sales are a must. Of course, tickets are also sold on the day of the event. Secure concentrated advertisements and mention in the area newspapers well in advance, to continue through the end of the event. You should also secure radio spots, free or as trade-outs. Having a disk jockey broadcasting on site and encouraging the public to attend the bazaar can be extremely effective. Publicity is needed to attract vendors as well as the general public. Invitations to appropriate music groups should be extended well in advance. The nonprofit nature of the sponsoring organization should be highlighted in all advertising.

Time: The fall bazaar usually lasts a weekend, Friday through Sunday. However, some groups hold bazaars that last 3 to 7 days, from 4 p.m. to midnight. Planning time can consume between 6 and 8 months. Set aside at least 2 to 3 days for setup; cleanup efforts will consume an entire day even with advance planning.

Expenditures: There are numerous expenses involved in this project; plan on spending at least $750 to get this event off the ground. This money will go toward renting the grounds, securing materials for the construction of booths, providing tents and portable toilets, hiring musical groups, advertising in the local media, and printing flyers. Naturally, great effort should be expended to obtain services and items as donations or trade-outs or at reduced prices. An example of a trade-out is a local radio station or area penny-saver newspaper receiving 100 free admission tickets and a free display area in exchange for free advertising and printed materials. You may have to pay to secure some musical groups; others will donate their time and effort. It is important to have groups that are popular with the general public. These groups will serve as great advertisement for the bazaar and represent money well spent. As the popularity of the bazaar increases each year, you will find that many musical groups will perform for free.

Personnel (Staff/Volunteers):   This event requires a large number of personnel: 75 volunteers and 5 to 10 staff. Volunteers should be organized into a number of teams under skilled leadership in order to accomplish all of the tasks that will make this bazaar a success. Adequate security is also a matter of concern, and both fire and police protection must be provided. Notify fire and police authorities well in advance, and ask for their assistance and suggestions. Frequently, they will station personnel on site if the event is large and sponsored by a nonprofit group.

Risk Management

The financial risks assumed revolve around two factors. First, the sponsoring group must be able to attract sufficient participants: quality musical groups, experienced food vendors, and craftspeople. Second, there must be sufficient ticket sales to provide a profit. The financial risks can be enormous if you do not properly organize the event. Keep cash expenditures to a minimum until advance ticket sales indicate that the bazaar will be a financial success. Another risk-management technique is to secure a business or individual to act as an "insurer," guaranteeing to make up any deficit. Check the insurance coverage for the site where the bazaar will be held to be sure it is adequate for this type of event.

Permits/Licenses

The local municipal governing body might require individual food and peddler's permits for exhibitors and vendors as well as a general license for the bazaar itself. Contact the local health department and the municipal offices (town clerk and bureau of licenses) to determine exactly what permits and permissions you need.

Hints

This fundraiser has the potential for wide community involvement, especially when the nonprofit sponsoring organization is highly thought of by those in the community. Securing businesses as sponsors helps to offset the financial risk and brings instant recognition and respectability to the event. Once this event has taken place and is well received, subsequent attempts to hold it will be much easier, because of the valuable experience your group will have gained coupled with the satisfied customer base that will have been created. The bazaars to be held in subsequent years will most likely be highly anticipated. Pick a date by which you can call a halt to the whole project without incurring significant expenses. By a specific date, examine advance ticket sales, projected income from the food and merchandise vendors, and acceptances of the invitations extended to musical groups, and decide whether it is prudent to continue with the plans for the bazaar.

Coaching Clinic of Champions

52

Potential Net Income

$10,000

Complexity/Degree of Difficulty

High

Description

This fundraising project involves staging an athletic coaching clinic, Friday afternoon and all day Saturday (and possibly Sunday morning and/or afternoon), primarily for coaches, although athletes are welcome as well. Invited guest speakers are coaches whose teams have won state championships or other prestigious tournaments as well as coaches with regional or even national reputations. The clinic's format involves lectures, demonstrations, and even field or game situations (if the clinic site includes a field or gymnasium). Profit is generated by charging an estimated 200 to 250 participants a $45 registration fee, thereby generating $9,000 to $11,250 gross profit. Additional profits can be generated from concessions and the sale of merchandise (souvenir T-shirts, hats, etc.). Or, you might be able to increase the admission price in your area. Finally, 8-foot by 8-foot display areas may be rented for $100 to $250 each to vendors who display equipment and supplies normally purchased by sports teams and coaches. Ten vendor tables will generate $1,000 to $2,500 in profit. Attendees must arrange for their own lodging and meals.

Scheduling

The clinic, which lasts 1-1/2 to 2-1/2 days, takes place prior to the start of the season, when the excitement is greatest.

Resources

Facilities: A school gymnasium may be used, or a strategically placed hotel with large conference rooms can be an attractive site. The advantage of the hotel site is that those attending the clinic who seek overnight accommodations (at an additional cost) will be able to stay at the clinic site. This facilitates late night and early morning brainstorming sessions among the attendees and speakers. Additionally, spouses and children of attendees can accompany them and take advantage of recreation facilities available at the hotel. The disadvantage of the typical hotel site is the absence of a gymnasium or field. Lodging and meals for the speakers should be obtained on a donated basis (from local hotels, bed-and-breakfasts, and restaurants).

Equipment and Supplies: Advertisement materials to be included in a mass mailing, stationery, registration and evaluation forms, and postage will be needed. You will need a notebook to keep your records in. Secure audiovisual equipment necessary for presentations as well as equipment and supplies used in the sport. Seek all such equipment as donations or loans from area schools or sporting goods companies. Tables and chairs must be provided. Also, complimentary notebooks or binders and other souvenirs should be distributed to those in attendance; usually, vendors who rent display space will donate items to be used as gifts or prizes. Of course, if concession items are to be sold, appropriate equipment and supplies must be secured.

Publicity and Promotion: Extensive advance publicity is required over a wide geographical area. Advertisements in coaching publications and mass mailings to schools and sport organizations within the geographical target area will help generate attendees. On-site registrations should be 5% to 10% higher than advance reservations.

Time: Planning begins 8 to 12 months in advance. Promotional activities should be initiated at least 8 months prior to the event with periodic reminders sent to prospective attendees. Setting up for the clinic will take 3 to 4 hours. Allow 2 to 3 hours for cleaning up after the clinic is over. The event itself runs 1-1/2 to 2-1/2 days.

Expenditures: Up to $500 must be expended up front for advance publicity and advertisements in appropriate sports publications. The eventual cost of the guest clinicians can run as high as $1,500 to $2,000. Be sure all contracts for guest speakers or clinicians are contingent upon the coaching clinic actually taking place; a final decision should be made some 4 to 6 weeks prior to the event as to whether the clinic will be a go.

Personnel (Staff/Volunteers):   Some 35 to 40 volunteers as well as 1 or 2 staff members are necessary to solicit vendors to rent space and to seek donations of all types (prizes, awards, use of facilities, free meals, lodging, and advertisements). Frequently, clinic speakers will agree to participate for $100 to $200 plus room and board (and perhaps mileage). Others may be willing to donate their time and expertise and will require room and board only. Commitments must be obtained 4 to 6 months in advance from various coaches who will serve as speakers or presenters for the clinic. If a big-name clinician is desired, be prepared to pay $500 and up plus expenses for a brief appearance.

Risk Management

If the clinic is held at a school or recreation facility, find out if the organization's regular insurance policy will cover the event. If not, it will be necessary to secure appropriate insurance. The greatest risk faced is financial. That is, will there be sufficient attendance not only to cover the expenses but to provide a tidy profit? To prevent a financial disaster, don't commit to paying the clinicians or the rental (if any) for a facility until you have a near break-even number of enrollees. Advance registration (at a discount) should be encouraged. Additionally, secure the financial backing of an individual or business that will promise to cover any losses, should they occur.

Permits/Licenses

If concessions are to be provided, check with the local health department and the office of the town clerk for permit requirements and health code standards and regulations.

Hints

Establish a cutoff date at which time it will be decided whether the plans should continue for the clinic. Establish in advance the amount of preregistration fees needed by a specific date. It is suggested that the coaching clinic be underwritten (sponsored) by one or more local companies or organizations, which will provide much, if not all, of the up-front capital needed to get the project off the ground. Be sure to thank the vendors, sponsors, and speakers who helped make the clinic a success. Similarly, thank those who attended and hand out evaluation forms to solicit opinions and suggestions. Finally, once the initial sport coaching clinic is successful, subsequent clinics will tend to be even more successful.

Part IV

Fundraisers Generating Over $10,000

Fundraiser 59.

Publishing a Cookbook

53

Potential Net Income
$12,000

Complexity/Degree of Difficulty
Moderate

Description
Recipes are gathered and published in a cookbook that is then sold throughout the community. A typical cookbook might be a spiral-bound, soft-cover publication; contain 100 to 250 recipes; and sell for $15. The cookbook can be divided into many different sections, such as appetizers and sandwiches; soups and salads; seafood, meats, and poultry; vegetables; casseroles; breads and rolls; low-calorie and low-fat dishes; desserts, including pies, pastries, cakes, and cookies; and beverages.

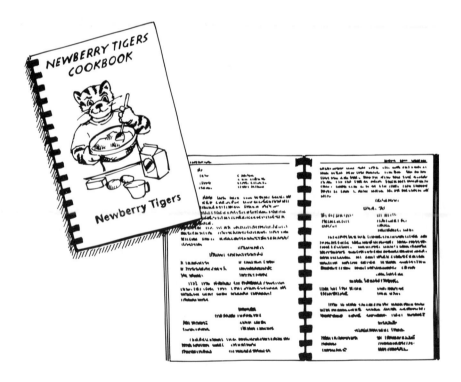

Scheduling

The cookbook project can be implemented any time of the year.

Resources

Facilities: This project requires a site where the cookbook can be put together, and a place for storing the finished product.

Equipment and Supplies: A computer (with word processing software) is a great aid in the writing and organizing of the cookbook. With the right software, the entire cookbook, along with illustrations, can be completed on a personal computer. The computer can also create order forms and record sheets to keep track of sales and inventory.

Publicity and Promotion: Refer to Fundraiser 54. Publicity will include solicitation of recipes as well as the actual marketing, selling, and distribution of the cookbooks. The books can be promoted by being displayed and sold in area businesses, at games, and at other special events sponsored by the group.

Time: Gathering and organizing recipes and printing the cookbooks can take up to 2 months. The major sales effort can last from 3 to 4 weeks, although unsold cookbooks can remain on sale until all are sold.

Expenditures: Because a sizable expenditure is required to produce the cookbooks, it is suggested that advance sales be conducted to reduce downside financial risks. In this case, the money is collected when the book is ordered. If the books cost $3 each to publish and your organization orders 1,000 cookbooks, there is an initial risk of $3,000. But if all of the 1,000 books are sold for $15 each, your organization will have made a tidy profit, $12,000. If the selling price is only $10, the profit is less ($7,000), which is still substantial. Naturally, the greater the number of books printed, the lower the individual cost per book. Seed money to get the project going will be around $200.

Personnel (Staff/Volunteers):   Some 25 to 30 volunteers and 2 to 5 staff members must be very active in both soliciting recipes and selling the cookbook. You will need a skilled proofreader-editor and organizer to arrange the contents of the book after the recipes are collected. An individual who is skilled with computers and appropriate software is invaluable.

Risk Management

The success of this fundraiser depends on the ability of volunteers and staff members to sell the cookbooks. The financial risk is the expenditure for the printing of the books. One way to handle some of this risk is to generate advance sales before the book is published. A sizable majority of the individuals who donate recipes will want to buy a book, especially if their names are included in the book. Thus, with 200 donated recipes there should be an automatic 100 to 150 advance sales, which would net an excellent prepublication gross profit of some $1,500—more than half of the $3,000 needed to pay for the entire lot of books (1,000 books at $3 per book). Stress that only original recipes should be submitted for the cookbook. You would not want to publish as an original a recipe that had been copied from a book or magazine.

Permits/Licenses

Selling the cookbooks door-to-door may require a peddler's license in some areas. The town clerk or the village or municipal governmental offices will be able to provide information about such requirements.

Hints

There are several national and regional publishing companies (so-called vanity presses—check the yellow pages of large cities under *publishers*) that specialize in publishing, for a fee, personalized books for individuals and organizations. Your organization may want to tie in with one of these firms to obtain assistance in creating and publishing a suitable product that will generate significant income. Or, you might check with the print shops at local colleges and universities to see what they will charge to print and bind the cookbook. Many will quote very reasonable prices if they can do the work during a down time at their presses. Finally, there is always the possibility of securing a sponsor who will help underwrite the cost of publishing the cookbook. Thus, almost all income becomes profit.

Selling a Souvenir Sport Publication

54

Potential Net Income

$13,000

Complexity/Degree of Difficulty

Moderate

Description

A publication is created that summarizes the history of your organization (whether it's a sports program, recreation department, or other nonprofit organization). The publication, which contains a pictorial and written historical account of the entity, is marketed to all possible constituencies of the organization as well as to the general public. Compiling, editing, and publishing the booklet (or significant parts of it) can be completed within the school or organization itself. Or, the project can be farmed out to professional publishers or printers; of course, the cost is significantly greater in this case.

Scheduling

This is a one-time fundraising effort, since it brings together in one document all of the information concerning the organization from its conception to the present. The actual marketing and selling of the publication can be scheduled at any time during the year. The sales period can last until the supply is exhausted.

Resources

Facilities: An area in which the organization can collect and file material and work on the project is necessary. You will also need secure storage space to hold the unsold publications.

Equipment and Supplies: A suitable camera with film is necessary if current photographs are to be taken. Old photographs will also greatly enhance the publication and its marketability. Access to historical data and photographs is absolutely essential. Mock covers can be used to promote the book, and order forms will also be needed.

Publicity and Promotion: Extensive prepublication publicity and promotion must be implemented. Mock covers can be printed and displayed at strategic locations within businesses in the community and in the school or recreation building. Prepublication orders (at a discount) should be encouraged. Place ads in school publications, and arrange for announcements to be made at all sporting and other related events. Individuals who are mentioned in the publication or whose photographs are to be included are prime candidates to purchase copies for themselves and their friends and associates. Other potential buyers are relatives of those who are included in the publication. The booklet should be marketed in terms of the value of the publication itself (as a historical reference and public relations piece) and on the basis of how the profits will be used to help the current recreation or sports program.

Time: Once the finished product is on hand, the concentrated selling window should be relatively short (2 to 3 weeks). However, the publication should remain on the market until all copies are sold. Taking advance orders will help you to order the appropriate number of booklets.

Expenditures: Expenditures will be determined by a variety of factors, such as the number of booklets to be printed, the number of pages, the quality and size of paper used, the type of cover chosen, the number of photographs, the type of binding, the number of services that can be obtained as donations or at reduced cost, and the cost of advertising. Although total downside risk can approach $3,000, using money from advance sales will reduce this. Plan on spending at least $100 before advance sales come in to get the project off the drawing board.

Personnel (Staff/Volunteers):   You will need 15 to 30 volunteers to collect and organize the contents of the booklet plus 30 to 40 volunteers organized in sales teams. This sales force can include anyone who has been adequately trained in how to approach potential purchasers. All professional assistance in respect to the creation of copy, layout, and printing should be sought on a donated basis or at a reduced cost, if possible.

Risk Management

The worst-case scenario is that there will be significant errors or omissions within the finished product. To prevent this, obtain professional and conscientious (but donated) assistance in the planning, collecting, editing, proofing, and printing processes. To reduce the risk of financial disaster, attempt to sell advance orders for the souvenir publication so that at least the cost of putting the piece together is covered before you spend money for printing. Proper selection and training of the selling corps will reduce the liability exposure associated with youngsters being involved in accidents or being injured. To reduce legal liability exposure, be sure to get permission before including any copyrighted materials and photographs.

Permits/Licenses

A peddler's license may be required in some communities if the souvenir booklets are sold door-to-door; check with the local municipal offices.

Hints

Refer to Fundraiser 53. Seek free or discounted services in terms of printing, photography, and advertising in an effort to reduce financial risk. The booklet must be sold for a reasonable profit yet the price must not be prohibitive. The key issues you must consider are (a) what the market will bear in terms of selling price, (b) how many copies you can reasonably expect to sell, and (c) the printing cost per copy. If 1,000 copies of the souvenir booklet are printed for $2 each and sold for $15 each, the profit comes to $13,000. If only 500 are sold for $15 each and the cost per booklet is $5, the profit shrinks to $5,000. Additional profits are possible if you obtain sponsorship contributions or sell advertisements within the publication itself.

Selling Advertising Space in a Facility

55

Potential Net Income

$15,000

Complexity/Degree of Difficulty

Moderate

Description

Large spaces in the sponsoring organization's facility (basketball, baseball, softball, soccer, football, etc.) are set aside for paid advertisement by various businesses. Space can be rented on a seasonal basis for whatever the market will bear. If 30 such spaces can be rented for $500 each (plus the cost of the signs or banners) per year, the potential annual profit is $15,000. The business that rents a space also pays for its sign, which must be approved by the organization.

Scheduling

The marketing of the available space should be initiated well before the sport season begins. This is to allow time for the construction of the signs and banners.

Resources

Facilities: The project requires space within an indoor or outdoor facility. Signs and banners can be placed on scoreboards, along walls of a building, or on fences surrounding playing fields; they can even hang from rafters. The dimensions of the spaces can vary, but they should be large enough to be seen by all spectators.

Equipment and Supplies: The signs containing the advertising messages must be expertly created or purchased (preferably at a reduced price). The data outlining the advertising program should be packaged, with an order form, in a professional-looking binder; photographs of the facility are extremely helpful in selling the concept. This kit can be a positive selling tool and should explain in detail the advantages accruing to both the advertiser and the school or recreation program. It is essential to provide specific demographics about spectators at various events held within the facility so that businesses will know their target audience and information about the overall purposes of the sponsoring organization.

Publicity and Promotion: This project can be marketed on the basis of potential advertising benefits accruing to the businesses as well as on the basis of the contribution to a worthy cause. Influential supporters of the organization should contact decision makers within the businesses that have been targeted as potential advertisers. The presentation kits should be a big help in marketing the spaces.

Time: There are minimal time requirements; typically, the planning time can be as long as 2 to 3 weeks, during which prospective customers can be identified. The selling window might be 2 to 3 weeks, with another 10 to 14 days set aside for the creation and placement of the signs.

Expenditures: The major expenses will be the creation of the signs or banners ($50 to $100 each), which are paid for by the advertisers. You should not need more than $200 to initiate this fundraiser.

Personnel (Staff/Volunteers):   This project requires influential volunteers, so-called centers of influence, who have access to business leaders who might agree to advertise in your facility. The sales team can be as few as 3 to 5 people or as many as 10 to 15 or higher, depending upon how many spaces are to be sold.

Risk Management

The appropriateness of the signage must be double-checked; all signs and advertisements must conform to the standards of the community and the sponsoring organization. There are few financial risks in this project because the major expenditures (for signs) have been paid for in advance. Do not order the signs to be made until you have a firm commitment from advertisers (or cash in hand). There are no significant liability risks in this fundraiser.

Permits/Licenses

Some communities may impose limitations on outdoor signage in terms of size, distance from the road, lighting, or other factors. Information regarding such limitations can be secured from the local zoning office or from the town clerk.

Hints

If advertisers balk at the idea of paying for the signs, you will have to build the cost of the sign into the overall cost; that is, the cost of the advertising space would be $550 or $600. It is also imperative that administrators of the sport or recreational organization approve of the advertising concept as well as the actual content or wording of the advertisements. Alcohol, tobacco, and some personal care products may not be appropriate for all sponsoring organizations and all communities.

Casino Royale

56

Potential Net Income

$15,000

Complexity/Degree of Difficulty

High

Description

Bringing the thrills of Las Vegas to the community (plus some profit to the sport or recreation group) is the aim of this fundraising event. Profit is generated from the admission price to the "Casino Royale" as well as from sales of "play money" and plastic poker chips that patrons can use at the various gaming tables. When the evening is drawing to a close, an auction of various donated merchandise is held. Patrons with winnings get to use the play money to purchase the auctioned items. A cash bar, concessions, or both provide still another profit center for the recreation or sport group. Concessions can be prepackaged, donated food or food that is prepared at the site. The food and drinks can vary from simple to sophisticated and can be used to continue a specific theme of the casino.

Scheduling

The event should be scheduled on either a Friday or Saturday evening.

Resources

Facilities: A large indoor facility, such as a gymnasium, auditorium, field house, or private "party house," will do nicely. A secure site should be selected to store the donated prizes until they are needed.

Equipment and Supplies: This event requires gaming equipment and supplies, which can be purchased or rented, as well as a secure site to store the money collected from the patrons. Appropriate decorations and gambling attire for volunteers certainly add a flavor of authenticity. If there is to be a cash bar, an appropriate array of refreshments must be secured. If concessions are to be available, it is necessary to secure cooking, warming, and dispensing equipment. Large tables should be secured to display the auction items. A microphone and sound system are required for the master of ceremonies. Signs can be made to promote the event ahead of time and to explain house rules the night of the event. You will also need play money, tickets, displays and posters, and a notebook for keeping accurate records of expenses and profits.

Publicity and Promotion: Publicity must be extensive and should involve air and print media as well as displays and posters positioned in area businesses. Advance tickets should be sold; publicize the fact that tickets sold at the door will be priced slightly higher (5% to 10%).

Time: Planning the event and collecting donated items will take 4 to 6 weeks. Additional lead time may be necessary if you wish to hire an outside expert to run the actual program. Advertising and promotion should take place during a 2-month period. You will need 4 to 6 hours to set up equipment, supplies, and decorations. The "Casino Royale" itself involves some 5 to 6 hours (7 p.m. to midnight or 1 a.m.). Set aside 2 hours to train the volunteers who will staff the gaming tables, and allow 2 to 3 hours for cleanup after the event.

Expenditures: Expenditures will go toward an extensive publicity campaign, plus purchase or rental of gaming equipment. If an outside expert or company is contracted to actually run the affair there will naturally be a cost for this service. Initial costs to get this event off the ground will be under $1,000.

Personnel (Staff/Volunteers):   About 25 to 40 volunteers and 3 to 5 staff from the sponsoring organization must be adequately trained to operate the various games and to run the concession stand and cash bar. There must also be a volunteer who is knowledgeable about all games of chance and who will have the authority and responsibility to settle all disputes, answer all questions, and conduct on-site lessons or workshops for the patrons who desire more information.

Risk Management

There are financial risks and public relations risks involved in this money-maker. Up-front money must be spent for advertising, supplies, and, if desired, a gambling expert to help oversee and direct the entire evening. It is also absolutely essential that adult volunteers be present throughout every area of the evening's activities to ensure that all activities are professionally conducted. All money paid to the casino's bank must be strictly accounted for and safely stored. Accurate financial record keeping remains of the highest priority. Be sure that liability insurance coverage is provided by the site owner's blanket liability policy. Having a cash bar necessitates additional precautions. Post signs that no one under the legal age will be served alcoholic beverages, and have bartenders check patrons' identification. Encourage patrons to choose designated drivers when the night is still young, but have backup arrangements for rides home with volunteers or a cab company.

Permits/Licenses

Local and state ordinances may require your group to secure a game of chance permit or a license permitting gambling. Check with the town clerk or office of permits where the event is to be held. A representative of the local law enforcement agency should be able to direct you to the state office that regulates gambling activities within the state, if indeed such activity is permitted at all. A state and/or local liquor license for the cash bar must be secured. Similarly, the concession area might be subject to licensing regulations depending upon whether the group cooks food on site or sells prepackaged, donated food.

Hints

You can organize the fundraising activities yourself or secure the services of a company or an individual who, for a price, will provide a complete casino night package. Such an agreement frequently includes all equipment and supplies as well as a gambling expert to provide demonstrations of slight-of-hand card tricks and to instruct both the general public and those staffing the tables in the fine art of gambling. Advance ticket sales are encouraged to give you some idea of the number of patrons likely to attend. Naturally, all personnel working the tables should be appropriately dressed in gambling attire. Finally, adequate signs should be displayed throughout the facility that outline succinctly but fully the rules of the house.

Car Raffle

57

Potential Net Income

$15,000

Complexity/Degree of Difficulty

Moderate

Description

An automobile (antique, vintage, or new) is raffled for $5 a ticket or three tickets for $10. The winner need not be present to win.

Scheduling

The car raffle can be scheduled for any time of the year. The sites chosen for selling tickets are important—set up ticket booths at various malls on the weekends to take advantage of increased foot traffic. A weekend is also an excellent time to conclude the raffle. Of course, displaying the vehicle at a popular indoor mall is an extremely effective marketing method.

Resources

Facilities: An area with a large amount of foot traffic is essential. A popular indoor mall is ideal. Displaying the vehicle, for the duration of the ticket sales period, in a highly visible area within a mall ensures that literally thousands of potential ticket buyers will see the vehicle daily. During peak shopping hours, if not all the time, there should be volunteers staffing the booth, selling the raffle tickets and talking about the sponsoring entity's achievements and goals.

Equipment and Supplies: A car to be raffled, booths or tables from which to sell the tickets, displays outlining some of the accomplishments and programs of the sponsoring group, and promotional signs, flyers, and posters are all essential components. Attractive tickets with stubs need to be printed. New vehicles as well as popular cars from the 1950s such as the '55-'58 Thunderbirds and the '56-'58 Chevrolets are very popular in this type of raffle. So too are Corvettes. Vintage vehicles, cars and trucks dated prior to 1950, are also extremely attractive. Of course, any vehicles can be used. The vehicles should be donated or obtained at a greatly reduced cost.

Publicity and Promotion: Tickets may be sold door-to-door and from various stores within the community. Orders for tickets can even be accepted by mail. Securing radio, print, and even television coverage for free or at a reduced cost increases the likelihood of greater ticket sales while keeping expenses down. Highlighting the worthiness of the sponsoring organization and how the money will be put to use is important. It is true that people will buy raffle tickets to have a chance to win the car, but they will also be contributing to the recreation or sport organization and its various projects. Use both motivations in the marketing and selling of tickets.

Time: No more than 60 days should be allowed for the sale of the raffle tickets. Allow longer than that and the process becomes boring. Planning for the event, making arrangements for the display of the automobile, and securing and refurbishing the vehicle (if needed) can take weeks, if not months, depending upon its condition. The raffle itself can be done in 15 minutes.

Expenditures: Having the vehicle donated is the best of all worlds; buying the car well below cost is good; and buying the vehicle at cost is acceptable but not preferable. The cost of the vehicle, if not donated, can run from as little as $2,500 for a rough version of a vintage vehicle to as high as $10,000 and beyond. The fundraising group should receive a discount, because this is a charitable fundraising project. The costs of the tickets and signs will run as high as $100 if they cannot be obtained gratis.

Personnel (Staff/Volunteers):   Volunteers are the bedrock of this project. A large sales force of 40 to 50 adults and youngsters is needed. Providing a range of prizes (donated, of course) for individuals who sell sizable numbers of tickets is an excellent motivating feature.

Risk Management

The worst-case scenario revolves around the financial risk involved in this project; specifically, insufficient tickets might be sold to cover the cost of the vehicle. To prevent this financial nightmare, secure an outright contribution from a benefactor or line up an insurance buffer, someone who guarantees to make up any difference between the vehicle's cost and the amount of money generated from ticket sales. Another area of concern centers around the integrity of the contest—it must be beyond question. Towards this end adults must supervise and conduct the actual drawing of the winning ticket. There are negligible risks in terms of legal liability because the blanket insurance policy held by the mall usually covers this type of event; check to be sure.

Permits/Licenses

Some states or communities require a permit to conduct a raffle. This is because a raffle is deemed to be gambling or is classified as a game of chance and thus falls under appropriate gaming laws and statutes. Check with the town clerk, municipal office, or city hall in the communities where the tickets are to be sold to determine whether any permits are required. If tickets are to be sold door-to-door, some communities also will require a hawker's or peddler's license.

Hints

Provide as many different ticket sales locations as possible. For example, local banks, car dealerships, grocery stores, or restaurants might all be willing to sell tickets. Also, door-to-door sales can be effective. Radio stations might take trade-outs in the form of free raffle tickets in exchange for advertising the raffle over the airwaves (the stations can in turn give the tickets away through radio contests). Scheduling a radio station's popular disk jockey to air a radio show directly from the mall on the day of the drawing enhances public relations and publicity. Publicize the winner and take color photographs of the drawing, the winner being handed the key, and the winner driving the car away. These photos can help promote and publicize next year's raffle.

Selling Bricks for a Memorial Sidewalk/Patio

Potential Net Income

$15,000

Complexity/Degree of Difficulty

High

Description

A memorial sidewalk or patio is paved with clay or concrete bricks on which the names of individual donors or businesses are permanently engraved. The engraved bricks may be purchased from a number of specialty manufacturers for approximately $15 to $18 each plus shipping. For a donation of $30, $50, or $75, whatever the market will bear, donors can have their names engraved on individual bricks that are placed in the sidewalk or patio.

Scheduling

This fundraiser works best when the weather is accommodating so that the bricks can be laid shortly after the conclusion of the sales campaign.

Resources

Facilities: This project requires a suitable site for storage of the engraved bricks before their permanent installation. Of course you will need an area where the bricks can be permanently laid.

Equipment and Supplies: Appropriate bricks and brick-laying equipment and supplies are required. The brick manufacturer can supply free brochures to be used in soliciting sales. Posters and flyers can be used as advertisement. Order forms will need to be printed. You will also need access to phones, preferably where there will be no charge for the calls, even long-distance ones.

Publicity and Promotion: A professional brochure, available from the specialty brick manufacturer, can be used as the selling tool both in person-to-person sales and in a mail campaign. A phone marathon may be conducted to reach alumni and friends both in and outside of your geographical area. The objective is to make it as easy as possible for the contributor to purchase an engraved brick. Ask local businesses to take orders and money for the engraved bricks on behalf of the sponsoring organization.

Time: Planning this fundraiser can take 1 to 2 weeks. The selling window can last 3 to 4 weeks if a sufficient number of volunteers are involved. The time needed for construction of the sidewalk or patio will vary in light of the project's complexity.

Expenditures: Each engraved brick costs around $15 to $18 (plus shipping). Thus, 1,000 bricks will cost in the neighborhood of $15,000 to $18,000. The bricks need not be purchased from the manufacturer until money has been collected from advance sales. Seek bricklayers who will donate their time and expertise. Use the phones at the school, or at a business that will not charge you for their use. Finally, there will be expenses for posters and flyers used in local marketing and promotional efforts. This project can be initiated with less than $500 in seed money.

Personnel (Staff/Volunteers): The project requires 1 to 2 professional bricklayers and 30 to 45 volunteers to sell the bricks. Some of these volunteers can also assist the bricklayers as they create the walkway or patio.

Risk Management

To reduce liability, secure professional bricklayers to install the bricks in the walkway or patio. It is better to have the job done properly than to find out too late that the bricks are coming loose because of poor workmanship (an accident can occur as a result). Those selling the bricks should emphasize that the names are engraved (not etched) into the bricks so that they can be read even after many years of exposure to weather. There is little financial risk when advance sales are made. Similarly, the legal liability exposure of the project principally rests in the construction of the walkway or structure. Ensure that the insurance policy covering the site is adequate. Finally, the professional bricklayers should be bonded and possess insurance.

Permits/Licenses

Local building codes must be adhered to in the planning and construction of the sidewalk or patio. The local building inspector's office or the municipal zoning department will be able to provide the necessary information relative to permits and licenses.

Hints

This is an excellent method of raising money and is a positive and long-lasting promotional effort as well. The bricks should be ordered all at the same time, in lots of 1,000. Of course, money is collected from the donors before the order is placed for the bricks. Other physical structures, such as walls, can also be built with these clay or concrete bricks; only your imagination limits the possibilities.

Summer Amusement Carnival   *59*

Potential Net Income

$15,000

Complexity/Degree of Difficulty

High

Description

A professional touring carnival is contracted by your group to provide traditional mechanical amusement rides. Your group provides animal rides, food concessions, entertainment, and souvenirs. The profit comes from the sale of tickets, concessions, and souvenirs. Ticket prices will depend on what the market will bear in your area. Additionally, corporate or business sponsorships are sought to help defray expenses and to ensure that a minimum amount of money is generated before the carnival opens. The carnival organization is responsible for erecting various amusement rides and for media advertising for the event.

Scheduling

The carnival is scheduled during the summer to take advantage of excellent weather and school holidays. Check with professional entertainment companies or agents (the yellow pages in any metropolitan phone book) for a list of various carnival companies.

Resources

Facilities: A large outdoor area suitably zoned for such a commercial enterprise is an absolute requirement. Additionally, adequate parking and access to utilities are equally important. Heavy foot and vehicular traffic near the amusement rides will generate big profits because of drop-in patrons. A large parking lot adjacent to a mall or school facility could be utilized with positive results.

Equipment and Supplies: The touring amusement group should provide all necessary equipment and supplies associated with the mechanical rides, including rope, stakes, and portable fences to restrict unauthorized access to specific areas. However, the local sponsoring group will need to provide an extensive amount of equipment and supplies in terms of concessions equipment, trash containers, display booths, items needed for animal rides, hats and T-shirts for volunteer security, prizes for sales-people, tickets, a ticket booth with change, and so forth. Flyers and signs can be made for additional promotional efforts.

Publicity and Promotion: Both advance and day-of-event ticket sales are encouraged through extensive print and airwave coverage. Volunteers should be organized into selling teams (with donated prizes awarded for the highest amount of sales) in order to increase the number of advance sales. Advertising displays provided by the carnival organization and placed in area businesses will provide additional publicity as will flyers distributed to area residences and placed on cars in parking lots. Large but tasteful signs placed strategically along area streets on the days of the carnival will help attract customers.

Time: You may need 6 to 7 months for planning, which includes reserving the touring amusement company and contracting for the use of the facility. Setup time by the professional carnival staff can be as little as 1 to 2 days. The carnival can last anywhere from 4 days to a week or beyond. Breakdown and cleanup will consume an entire day.

Expenditures: Try to obtain use of the facility for free, due to the nonprofit nature of the sponsoring organization and the worthiness of the fundraising project. The professional carnival group will contract for either a flat fee or a percentage of the gross income. Plan on spending upward of $500 in seed money, which will go toward advertising (other than in the media) and printing.

Personnel (Staff/Volunteers):   You will need 25 to 40 volunteers and 3 to 7 staff members to bring this project to fruition. These people will be involved in securing a site, securing donated equipment and supplies, lining up entertainment and musical groups to perform, selling tickets, obtaining corporate sponsorships, setting up the facility, providing security, and cleaning up afterward.

Risk Management

Be sure that your group has adequate insurance for this event. Check with legal counsel concerning the liability the group and its members might be exposed to in conducting such an event. Safety is of the utmost importance. Check to see the state license or permit of the carnival organization—most states now regulate amusement rides. Keep the site clean, and have adult volunteers, wearing identifiable T-shirts and hats, provide additional security and discourage roughhousing. Equally important is selling a sufficient amount of tickets. There are significant financial risks if insufficient tickets are sold to cover the cost of contracting the professional amusement company.

Permits/Licenses

Numerous licenses and permits must be secured before the carnival can open. The professional amusement company must also have appropriate insurance and meet the state, county, and community requirements for operating the various mechanical rides; insist upon receiving copies of all such permits. Food permits must be secured and all health requirements met in terms of preparing, storing, and selling food (check with the town clerk or licensing department).

Hints

Double-check the reputation and record of the professional amusement company before entering into an agreement. Also, identify a date by which you can cancel the agreement if insufficient advance tickets are sold. Consider securing sponsors (local businesses) to help defray expenses and to provide a parachute in terms of financial protection. Similarly, another nonprofit organization (such as a Rotary or Lions club) might be taken on as a partner in an effort to borrow respectability and decrease financial risk; of course, you must share profits with any partner.

Sports Dinner Catered by Athletes and Coaches

60

Potential Net Income

$15,000

Complexity/Degree of Difficulty

High

Description

A sit-down dinner is provided for 250 to 300 community people. The table servers are the athletes, coaches, and administrators from the sponsoring sports organization and other celebrities from the community, such as local radio and television personalities. Tickets for the affair go for $50 to $75, or whatever the market will support. The servers dress in tuxedos (borrowed) and perform various tasks in exchange for tips that are then donated to the sponsoring group; the servers compete to see how much money they can generate for the sponsoring organization. For example, a patron might pay $25 for an athlete's autograph or might contribute $35 if a server can talk a coach into doing an Irish jig or singing "Home on the Range" in front of the throng. Near the end of the evening the top two or three biggest tippers receive grand prizes, which might be a donated trip to Disney World (Florida), Cedar Point (Ohio), Six Flags (various locations), or Niagara Falls (Canada). Additionally, throughout the latter part of the dinner, a variety of prizes and souvenirs that have been donated by individuals, companies, and sports organizations are auctioned. Auction items can include sports equipment (balls, hockey sticks and pucks, helmets, gloves, etc.) from area sport standouts and from nationally known celebrities. Finally, a comedian is secured to entertain the audience during a 20- to 30-minute segment of the evening.

Scheduling

The dinner may be scheduled on any Friday or Saturday evening.

Resources

Facilities: A party house or other restaurant that can seat a large crowd is needed. Adequate and safe parking is also a must. An area set aside within the dining area where the auction can be held and the prizes displayed makes the evening go faster and highlights the auction items.

Equipment and Supplies: Prizes and auction items must be solicited from a whole host of donors, both local and national. An excellent sound system is mandatory. Tickets need to be provided to guests. Tastefully created signs and banners will lend class to this event.

Publicity and Promotion: News media coverage should provide wide exposure for this exciting event. The cocktail hour, evening meal, auction, tipping competition, and entertainment all help to promote the event and should be highlighted in the pre-event publicity. Don't forget to emphasize the worthiness of the sponsoring organization, the quality of the sport programs it provides, and the benefits for the community.

Time: Planning for the event will take 3 to 6 weeks. Soliciting and collecting the auction items will take another 3 to 6 weeks. Plan on the evening's activities to last 3 to 4-1/2 hours. The cocktail hour (cash bar) starts at 6:30 p.m. and will last 45 minutes to 1 hour, with the dinner to start promptly at the cocktail hour's conclusion. The final auction items should be put on the block around 9:30 p.m.

Expenditures: The services of a professional auctioneer and a talented comedian must be secured. The cost of the meal can vary widely (from $20 to $35 per plate) depending upon the type of food provided, the site of the dinner, and the extent to which the food can be secured free or at reduced cost. The tuxedos will be rented or borrowed for the event. Anticipate spending about $500 before any income is realized.

Personnel (Staff/Volunteers):   You will need 50 to 60 volunteers to solicit prizes and items for the auction, to promote the event, and to sell the advance tickets. The group of coaches, athletes, and administrators working the dinner can number 40 to 60. For each table of 10 people there should be at least 2 servers, so if 300 are in attendance with 10 to a table, there should be 60 servers. There may be some overlap among volunteers, so about 70 to 85 total volunteers should do.

Risk Management

Appropriate training of the servers and close attention to the preparation, storage, and distribution of the meals will significantly reduce liability risks. Anytime alcoholic beverages are involved in a fundraising event, the organizers must ensure that only individuals of legal age are given or sold alcohol. IDs must be checked, and alternative transportation arranged (e.g., cabs) for individuals who should not be driving. There is a risk in planning and promoting the event and making commitments to a variety of individuals without knowing whether sufficient tickets will be sold. Selling advance tickets reduces the financial risk. Once this fundraiser has been successful, its replication in subsequent years will prove to be less challenging.

Permits/Licenses

None are needed if the event is held in a restaurant or a party house that already possesses food and alcohol licenses.

Hints

Corporations and businesses that buy tickets in groups of 10 (there are 10 seats to each table) receive a discount on the price. Additionally, corporate sponsors are sought to help underwrite the evening's festivities (through the donation of money, prizes, services, and personnel). These sponsors are acknowledged with signs and banners that are strategically located throughout the dining area.

Antique and Custom Car and Truck Show

61

Potential Net Income

$15,000

Complexity/Degree of Difficulty

High

Description

An antique and custom car and truck show is held, with prizes awarded in a variety of categories. Those who pay to attend the show vote for awards in various categories. There is a modest charge ($5 for advance registration and $8 for on-site registration) for those displaying their vehicles. General admission charges are $3 for advance tickets and $5 on the day of the event. Children under the age of 7 are admitted free. Attendees are provided informational brochures that will help them locate the various types of vehicles and booths on the lot. Attendees use the ballots inserted into the brochures to vote for their favorite cars and trucks. An additional profit center revolves around a concession stand run by volunteers of the sponsoring organization. Another area for potential profit is the sale of souvenirs or car memorabilia; in this instance, an 8-foot by 8-foot space is rented for $50 to $75 to individuals or companies wishing to sell such items. A fourth source of income comes from selling advertising space in the brochure. Prime advertisers are car-related businesses, but other types of businesses should not be neglected. Parking for the general public is free. Volunteers, wearing distinctive T-shirts and hats, provide security.

Scheduling

The event should be held all day on a Saturday or Sunday, rain or shine. The judging of the vehicles takes place in the morning, no later than noon. In the afternoon the prizes are awarded at a formal ceremony.

Resources

Facilities: An outdoor site large enough to display between 300 and 500 antique and custom vehicles and to park 2,000 to 3,000 spectators' cars is required. Automobile dealers might welcome the opportunity to become involved if they have the space. Or, you can use a school's or recreation organization's general-purpose field or the blacktop parking area around your group's own site. A large mall parking lot, part of which can be roped off, can serve as an excellent site. The advantage for the owner of the commercial site used for the show is that thousands of people will walk through or near the business as they view the cars and trucks.

Equipment and Supplies: Concession equipment and supplies need to be secured. Also, commemorative plaques for all exhibitors and prizes for the winners of the different categories of cars and trucks need to be obtained, hopefully at a reduced cost or as part of a trade-out (the donor gets free advertisement within the show's brochure). Tents should be secured to house the concession operation, judging area (you will need tables and chairs here), and disk jockey equipment (if a disk jockey will be present). A microphone and an excellent outdoor speaker system are also required. Thus, adequate electrical power is a must. Use rope and stakes to mark off the whole area, as well as the individual spaces for booths. You will also need scorecards; tickets; postage; a mailing list of potential exhibitors, spectators, and vendors; and a cash box with change at the ticket booth. Use a computer, with appropriate software and a printer, to design brochures, ballots, flyers, and posters.

Publicity and Promotion: Advance publicity through the area media is essential. Convincing a local radio station to promote the event by having a popular disk jockey air the show on site is a big boon. Working out a trade-out agreement with the radio station can generate a lot of free, advance spots over the air waves. Mailing flyers to those who have participated in similar events in the past, as exhibitors, spectators, and vendors, can be quite successful. Placing posters or flyers in car-related businesses is also important.

Time: This is a one-day event, which can be held annually. Advance planning, especially the first time the show is held, can be as long as 3 to 5 months. Setting up for this show will take 4 to 6 hours; cleaning up can take 2 to 3 hours.

Expenditures: Securing prizes, advertising, and attracting sufficient numbers of display cars will be the major expenditures. Commemorative plaques to be given to vehicle owners taking part in the event must be donated or purchased. Printed brochures containing a list of all of the displayed vehicles (and the various categories of competition) plus advertising must be created. Selling ads for this printed piece can raise big money. Also, flyers, posters, and scorecards need to be purchased or made. It is expected that you will be able to secure the site for the car show without cost. There may be costs involved in publicizing efforts and in securing the tents, tables, and chairs. Rope and stakes should be purchased to rope off the area to ensure that no one walks into the display area without paying. Total initial costs will be around $750.

Personnel (Staff/Volunteers):   Some 30 to 45 staff and volunteers are needed to negotiate the use of a site, run the concession stand, take tickets, sell advertising, design printed pieces, supervise parking, organize and implement the judging of the vehicles, provide security, erect tents, and perform a host of other on-site tasks.

Risk Management

In terms of general liability, the site owner's general insurance policy may cover the event; be sure this is the case. There is a risk in terms of inclement weather, which is a risk you will have to assume; to be safe, set up tents for specific areas such as the concession and souvenir stands, the judges' work area, and the radio station broadcast area. Obtaining firm commitments from a large number of vehicle owners to attend the show is an absolute must; you can work through various car buff groups and attempt to secure commitments from the groups themselves that their members will be willing to display their vehicles. The sale of advance tickets will decrease the financial risks associated with this fundraising project.

Permits/Licenses

No special permits are usually required other than those associated with the concession stand. It is advisable to notify the local law enforcement agency so that officers can anticipate any changes in the normal traffic flow in the area. Sometimes officers will be willing to patrol the area on horseback and in vehicles, thereby providing additional security and assisting in traffic control.

Hints

All owners displaying their vehicles are given a beautiful 2-inch x 2-inch plaque to commemorate the car and truck show. It is important to restrict access to the exhibition area so that no one can just walk into the area. Also, security for the vehicles is very important, since many of them are worth thousands of dollars. Finally, there could be a "swap/sell" area set aside for the exchange of vintage car accessories.

Selling Coupon Books

62

Potential Net Income

$15,000

Complexity/Degree of Difficulty

High

Description

A book of coupons that offer steep discounts on an extensive list of purchases throughout the community is compiled and sold for $10 or $15. Merchants offering a variety of services and goods are solicited to take part in this fundraising project. The profit comes from the sale of the coupon booklets themselves. The merchants are motivated to take part in the coupon book project because of the advertising exposure, the possibility of attracting new business, and the opportunity to help a worthy sport or recreation organization or specific project. With the net profit per book hovering around $8 to $13, the sponsoring organization selling a mere 1,500 booklets can realize a $12,000 to $19,500 profit.

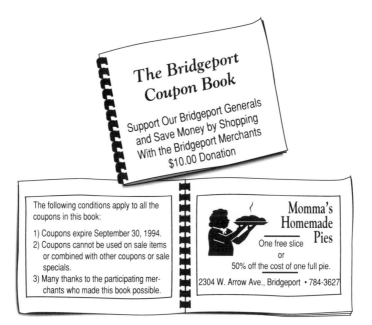

Scheduling

The sale of the coupon books can be scheduled at any time of the year. If extensive door-to-door selling is to take place, schedule the selling window during good weather.

Resources

Facilities: None are needed.

Equipment and Supplies: Order blanks must be developed that volunteers can use in gathering information from participating merchants. Create point-of-sale posters or flyers to display in businesses. Design the coupons via computer graphics using a computer, printer, and appropriate software; or solicit camera-ready designs from the businesses.

Publicity and Promotion: Person-to-person contacts by both youngsters and adults (with neighbors, friends, and relatives) make up the bulk of the promotional and selling activities. Selling the booklets at athletic contests or recreational events is also highly productive. Parents and friends frequently offer to take the booklets to work, where they can easily be sold. Asking area merchants to sell the booklets in their stores and display point-of-sale posters is recommended.

Time: Soliciting businesses to participate in this project will consume upward of 4 to 6 weeks. It will take another 2 to 3 weeks to design all of the coupons (frequently using the merchants' own logos). It may take 1 to 2 weeks for the coupon books to be printed and bound. The time set aside for general sales of the coupon booklets should not exceed 4 weeks; 90% of what can be sold will be sold within that time. What is left unsold at the end of the 4-week selling window should be given to the top sellers in a last-ditch attempt (1 week) to sell the remaining booklets. The coupons should be valid for 5 to 12 months after sales begin.

Expenditures: The major cost of the project is the development and printing of the booklets themselves at $2 per booklet, $3,000 total. Ask the printer to contribute by printing the booklet at cost or at a significantly reduced price.

Personnel (Staff/Volunteers):   You will need 2 or 3 volunteers skilled in graphic arts or in the use of computer graphics to create the artwork for the coupons. Similarly, 35 to 50 volunteers should be involved in soliciting merchants and selling the booklets.

Risk Management

The coupons must represent significant savings for the purchasers of the booklets. There should not be any free house appraisals offered by real estate firms or free insurance evaluations, because these are not really discounts. Be sure that the conditions of each discount as described on the coupon can be clearly understood by the merchant and by the purchaser of the booklet. To avoid misunderstandings and possible legal entanglements, merchants should sign a statement that outlines exactly what their coupons entitle the bearer to. It is imperative that each coupon contain an expiration date beyond which it will not be honored. This is usually some 5 to 7 months from the date when the booklet is available for purchase but can be as long as 12 months. And, the merchants should be told how many booklets are to be available for sale. There is a real financial risk involved in this fundraiser since the coupon books will have to be printed prior to being sold.

Permits/Licenses

Typically the sale of such booklets by a nonprofit group will not involve any permit or license unless the booklets are sold door-to-door. In that case, you may need to secure a peddler's or hawker's permit from the community licensing bureau.

Hints

The booklet should be approximately 6 inches by 2-1/2 inches in size and contain between 60 and 100 coupons (at a minimum) representing significant discounts and real savings. Some coupons might offer goods or services at half price or "two for the price of one" (e.g., haircuts, movie tickets, or dinners). Some coupons might represent a free service (car wash) or a special gift (a plastic flower) when a purchase of $5 is made at the local card shop. Other possibilities include an oil change for $7, a pizza with all the toppings for the cost of a plain cheese pizza, or a T-bone steak dinner for 25% off the regular price. If any coupon booklets are left over at the conclusion of the selling window, they can be given away as prizes at various athletic contests and school meetings. The important point here is that the booklets need to be distributed and the coupons used so that the merchants will be satisfied that their participation had a positive effect on the traffic pattern and the profit picture of their businesses.

Selling Pseudo Deeds

63

Potential Net Income
$20,000

Complexity/Degree of Difficulty
Moderate

Description
This is a make-believe situation in which a portion of the recreation or sport facility is "sold" to the general public. In actuality only a framed fake deed and a photo of the property are sold. The portion to be sold can be a square inch or a square foot of the football or baseball field, or a specific brick of the recreation building or field house. The fake deed should identify the specific item (the location of the square inch or the brick). If fake deeds are sold for $15 to $20 each, some $20,000 can be generated in net revenues in a minimum of time, with a minimum of downside risk and a minimum of effort.

Scheduling
This fundraiser can be scheduled any time during the year.

Resources
Facilities: Almost any indoor or outdoor facility will suffice. A room where the deeds and photos can be stored is necessary.

Equipment and Supplies: This requires professional-looking fake deeds giving ownership to a part of the athletic facility to the purchaser. Deeds can be inexpensively printed at any print shop. Inexpensive picture frames can be purchased in bulk. Similarly, multiple copies (from a negative) of a suitable color or black-and-white photo of the facility can be obtained for insertion along with the fake deed in the frame. You will need a 35-mm camera and film.

Publicity and Promotion: Publicity and promotion are what make this fundraising effort a success. Obtain free mention in the media, including published photographs of the facility and members of the group organizing the fundraising effort. Displaying sample deeds in various businesses where they may also be purchased is strongly recommended. Giving the buyers the framed photos and fake deeds is an excellent promotional tactic. The attractiveness of the fake deed and photo, which can be hung in the home or office as a souvenir, plus the fact that the money is going toward a worthy cause will motivate people to buy. Another promotional twist is to have some of the deeds or photos autographed by administrators, team members, or coaches. This can greatly enhance the value of the product and enable you to sell these versions for an additional $5 or $10 apiece.

Time: This fundraising campaign can be completed within 6 weeks. The key factor is to establish a specific amount of time for sales. Organizing the event itself can be completed in 2 to 3 days, while it may take up to 10 days to have the certificates created and printed. Certificates and photos can be framed as they are needed; you don't need to frame 1,000 deeds before you start to sell them.

Expenditures: The costs of the fake deeds, picture frames, and photographs are the major expenses. If the items are not donated, be prepared to spend approximately $1 per fake deed (photo, deed, and frame). To generate $20,000 in sales at $15 per deed, 1,333 deeds must be sold. However, initial seed money need not exceed $200. Profits from initial sales can be used to purchase additional frames and photos.

Personnel (Staff/Volunteers):   The sales team will consist of 35 to 50 volunteers and 1 to 3 staff members. Some of these individuals can also be involved in creating and designing the deeds themselves.

Risk Management

The deeds must state that the purchase does not actually transfer property, that is, that the donation is a contribution to a fundraising effort. There is limited financial risk involved in this fundraiser since the cost of the fake deeds is so minimal. Similarly, there is no real legal exposure as long as the deeds explicitly state that no real property is being sold.

Permits/Licenses

No permits are required for the overall fundraising activity. However, if volunteers attempt to sell the deeds door-to-door, a peddler's license might be required by local ordinances; check with the town clerk or the municipal office in charge of licenses.

Hints

Publicizing how the money to be raised will be used to benefit the community and the sport or recreation program is a key factor in this fundraiser. It is wise to obtain the services (free or not) of an excellent artist to design the deeds. Likewise, do not skimp on the quality of the paper, the photographs, or the printing of the deeds.Individuals will be more likely to purchase an impressive framed fake deed and photo.

Celebrity Sports Dinner

64

Potential Net Income

$20,000

Complexity/Degree of Difficulty

High

Description

A national or regional celebrity, one who will attract a large crowd, serves as the guest of honor for a sports dinner. The celebrity agrees to attend the dinner either for a fee or at no charge. The celebrity can be scheduled to provide a speech as well as sign autographs after the meal. Inviting two or more celebrities to participate would greatly enhance this event's attractiveness and marketability. Tickets are sold for $100 or $125 a plate or even more depending upon what is acceptable in your area. A table for 10 may be reserved by businesses and various organizations, including educational institutions, for a 10% or 15% discount.

Scheduling

The dinner can be scheduled on a Friday or Saturday evening at any time of the year.

Resources

Facilities: A sufficiently large dining area is required to accommodate 250 to 300 individuals; and ample and suitable parking is needed as well.

Equipment and Supplies: Items normally associated with a formal banquet and bar are required. An excellent sound system for the after-dinner speeches is a must. Tickets and posters for the event must be printed.

Publicity and Promotion: The purpose of the celebrity dinner, that is, the support of the nonprofit sport organization and sponsored programs, is a major selling point. All segments of the community might be viewed as potential ticket purchasers, so it is necessary to utilize radio and television as well as the print media in an effort to get the message across to the various publics. Depending upon who the celebrity is, the media might give the dinner coverage as either sports news or community news, thus providing additional free exposure. Having tickets available at selected businesses and organizations is a must. Trade-outs of tickets for advertisements and other services and goods can be very effective.

Time: The planning for this event should be initiated 6 to 9 months prior to the date of the event. Selling tickets can consume 3 to 4 weeks. It can take 2 to 3 hours to set up for this dinner. The festivities consume most of the evening, running from 6:30 p.m. to 9:30 or 10 p.m. Cocktails (cash or free bar) start at 6:30, while the dinner itself begins around 7 or 7:15 p.m. The presentation by the celebrity begins around 9 p.m. You will need 1 to 2 hours afterward to clean up.

Expenditures: There could be significant expenses ($3,000 to $7,000) associated in booking the national celebrity if the individual is not willing to donate his or her time and presence. The cost of the evening meal and alcohol (including the use of the site itself) will average $25 to $30 per person. Seed money can be as high as $750 for publicity and advertising.

Personnel (Staff/Volunteers):   A local television or radio announcer should be selected to serve as the master of ceremonies. You will need 35 to 50 volunteers and 3 to 10 staff members to market and sell the advance dinner tickets. Tickets are sold for this type of event through personal and professional contacts. The person-to-person approach to ticket sales is the key to meeting the sales quota.

Risk Management

The sales force, using professional and personal contacts, must sell a sizable number of advance tickets. In this way, even before the initial public announcement of the celebrity dinner a significant portion of the cost of the affair will be covered by pledges or ticket purchases. Whenever alcohol is served, especially if the alcohol is free, you must be extremely careful in terms of individuals becoming intoxicated. Providing designated drivers or cabs for those guests who should not be driving due to excessive alcohol consumption will help prevent legal liability exposure as well as create a positive public image.

Permits/Licenses

Permits for preparing and serving food must be secured, and all health regulations completely adhered to. A liquor license or permit is also necessary.

Hints

It may be possible to schedule a number of national celebrities to attend the same dinner. The price of the tickets is determined by two factors: who the visiting celebrities are, and what the market will bear. If the event draws 250 individuals at $100 a plate, you can generate a gross profit of $25,000. At $125 a plate the profit is even higher. This type of fundraising event can easily become an annual affair. Another method of organizing this celebrity dinner is to piggyback with another nonprofit, charitable organization, such as the March of Dimes, the YMCA, or Special Olympics. In this case both organizations sponsor the event, share in the work, and split the proceeds. Corporations and businesses may be approached to purchase tables (e.g., 10 tickets) or to help underwrite the cost of securing the celebrity (i.e., speaking and appearance fees and transportation and lodging costs).

Flea Market

65

Potential Net Income
$24,000

Complexity/Degree of Difficulty
High

Description
A large outdoor area is set aside each weekend (Saturday and Sunday) May through October for a flea market. Admission to the flea market is free to the public. The site is marked off in sections (e.g., 8 feet by 10 feet) that are rented to vendors for the display of their merchandise. The sites are rented for anywhere from $25 to $75 per weekend; the potential gross profit if an average of 50 vendors takes part is as high as $30,000. The net profit can easily approach $24,000 for the season.

Scheduling
The flea market is scheduled on weekends during the spring, summer, and fall; business hours are 9 a.m. to dusk. Anticipate that it will take one entire season to get the operation off the ground and make it minimally successful. It is best to err on the conservative side when making predictions regarding profitability of the event for the first year.

Resources
Facilities: A large area that is located close to a large population center yet provides easy access for motorists is necessary. Also, ample parking is absolutely essential. Try to secure the use of the site for free.

Equipment and Supplies: You can provide permanent or semipermanent booths as well as tables for the vendors, although many vendors will provide their own display tables. An adequate number of trash cans, portable toilets, and portable water dispensers will also be required. You will need first-aid supplies for a first-aid station. A sign that is visible from the roadway is necessary to provide on-site advertisement.

Publicity and Promotion: Extensive, ongoing advertisement in the newspapers and via the radio is recommended to ensure that the general public is aware of the flea market. Similarly, you must line up vendors to display their wares. Do this by contacting hobby and craft supply shops for lists of craftspeople and other potential vendors as well as by placing advertisements in the local newspapers.

Time: Initial planning can consume almost 9 months due to the nature of the fundraising effort and the large number of individuals who must be contacted. The event itself is held on a weekend. Plan to spend 1 to 2 hours to set up each day and 1 to 2 hours to tear down and clean up.

Expenditures: There may be sizable up-front expenditures in terms of advertisement and publicity. Set aside at least $2,000 with which to implement this fundraiser.

Personnel (Staff/Volunteers):   A sizable group of volunteers and staff, from 45 to 60, is required to make this event a success. Their first challenge, after a suitable site has been selected, is to contract with a sufficient number of appropriate vendors. Volunteers will be needed to facilitate parking at the flea market as well as to provide security and general supervision. As the operation expands and more people attend each weekend there will be a need to provide a first-aid tent and a volunteer certified in first aid and CPR.

Risk Management

During the first year it might be necessary to discount the amount charged to the vendors, because you are caught in a *catch-22*. That is, customers will not want to come to the flea market until there are a large number of vendors with a wide array of items for sale. On the other hand, vendors won't want to spend their time, much less their money, to set up their displays if there are not large crowds. Thus, in the early stages you must attempt to get as many vendors as possible. The financial risks can be sizable. You must ask yourself what competition you face, in the form of other flea markets located in the area. If the proposed flea market meets a need and there is little competition in the area the odds are in favor of the project. However, it doesn't hurt to have financial backers at the onset to minimize the financial risks. Liability insurance coverage must be secured for this type of event to protect the owner of the property if the site is privately owned and to protect the sponsoring organization and its staff and volunteers.

Permits/Licenses

Local ordinances will require a merchant's or business license for this type of event. Also, you must pay strict attention to local restrictions regarding safety and sanitary provisions. The local department of public health will help you determine which standards must be met and which permits secured.

Hints

Sport organizations should not undertake this type of fundraising effort unless all of the necessary ingredients are present that will allow the flea market to be a success. The climate and the timing for such a venture must be right. Also, volunteers and staff must realize that this is a long-term commitment in terms of work, money, and time. However, if the necessary tools and assets are present (people, facilities, site location, money, and climate), then the possibility of long-term financial success is real.

Triad Fundraising Evening
Raffle, Barbecue Dinner, and a Big-Time Sport Event Viewed on Big-Screen Television

Potential Net Income
$25,000

Complexity/Degree of Difficulty
High

Description
This triad fundraising evening involves a dinner, a raffle, and the opportunity to watch a premier sports event (such as the Super Bowl, World Series, NCAA basketball championship, or Wimbledon finals) on big-screen TVs—all for $100 per person (or more, depending upon what the market will bear). Ticket stubs for the evening festivities are placed in a large box and are drawn throughout the evening. The donated prizes are given away to the first 100 (or 125, or 150) ticket holders chosen at random. Both the raffle and the barbecue buffet begin an hour or so before the televised sporting event starts. After the game begins the raffle is stopped until halftime, when it will continue until the second half begins. After the sporting event, the rest of the items, if any, are raffled.

Scheduling
This is an annual event, held each year on the date of the specified athletic event. You may want to schedule it to take place in a school cafeteria, restaurant, or banquet hall.

Resources
Facilities: You must have access to a large dining room (your own facility or an establishment secured for this purpose) that can accommodate 250 to 300 or more people. Also, space must be secured where the raffle items can be stored until the day of the event.

Equipment and Supplies: You will need six to seven big-screen televisions, numerous donated raffle prizes, and display tables used to show off the items. Tickets for the evening must be printed. A good sound system is a must.

Publicity and Promotion: Extensive and consistent advance publicity is needed, especially for the first year of the event. Publicity should focus on the raffle and the dinner but should also emphasize the enjoyment and camaraderie of the evening. Tickets should be placed in strategic locations within the community and also hawked via print media and local radio. Highlighting the purpose for which the profits will be used can be a great motivating factor in ticket sales.

Time: Ticket sales should take place within a 3- to 4-week time period, no longer. Planning, and the collection, transportation, and storage of the donated items to be raffled, can consume as much as 11 to 12 months. Thus, as soon as the current "Triad Fundraising Evening" is over, planning for next year's event will begin; it takes that long to plan and organize all of the details. The event itself will last 5 to 6 hours.

Expenditures: Expenditures include the rental of the big-screen TVs (if they cannot be secured as donations) and the cost of the barbecue dinner. If the meal costs $10 per person and there are 300 in attendance paying $100 each, the profit can be in the neighborhood of $27,000 minus the cost of the television rentals. This fundraising project can be initiated with as little as $500. No expenditures for the TV rentals, food and drinks, or the facility rental (if any) will be made until the advance ticket sales indicate that the event will generate a profit and is therefore a "go."

Personnel (Staff/Volunteers):   The crucial element in this fundraiser is the personnel involved, some 40 to 50 volunteers and 2 to 5 professional staff members. Advance ticket sales must be completed on a timely basis. Individuals are also needed to collect and transport the various raffle items. And, of course, the staffing of the raffle event itself is crucial.

Risk Management

Any time food is involved there is the problem of how many reservations to confirm. You don't want to reserve too many meals or too few. To reduce the financial risk it is imperative that a deadline be established for ticket sales. At that point the reservations (plus 10%) can be confirmed with the food service or restaurant you have chosen. This helps to keep the financial risks manageable. In terms of legal risks, be sure to comply with all health and food regulations so as to ensure a safe environment for the event.

Permits/Licenses

You must adhere to the local and state regulations or ordinances governing gambling activities. Similarly, permits to provide food must be secured, and health regulations must be closely followed. Check with the town clerk or county licensing board as well as the state entity controlling games of chance to see whether special permits are required for this event. The local health office will be able to provide information regarding food licenses and health standards. If this event is held in a restaurant, you don't need to worry about food licenses because the restaurant will have already taken care of this task. Finally, you might need to get permission to show the sporting event during this fundraiser from the organizers of the event itself, from the television network broadcasting the event, or from both.

Hints

This fundraiser tends to grow more successful year after year. When people enjoy themselves they tend to return, and when satisfied they also help spread the word to others. Word of mouth can be extremely effective advertising. In no time at all this event can become "the event" in the community and a mainstay in the sport organization's fundraising arsenal.

Demolition Dividends

67

Potential Net Income
$27,500

Complexity/Degree of Difficulty
High

Description
Selling pieces of a facility that has been demolished is the key to this fundraiser. For example, when a field house is demolished, the bricks are sold (with a metal plate attached to each stating that it came from the old field house) to the general public for $20 to $25. If artificial turf is being replaced, sections of the old turf can be cut into 8-inch or 12-inch squares, placed in picture frames with engraved metal plates attached, and sold as souvenirs for $20 to $35 each or whatever the local market will bear. Ditto with wooden flooring that is being torn up. It takes only 1,500 bricks or wooden souvenirs sold at $20 apiece to gross $30,000.

Scheduling
This fundraiser is dependent upon part of a facility being demolished and remnants being available for the group to sell.

Resources
Facilities: The project requires any facility that is being torn down and thus can serve as a source of physical objects that can be "dressed up" and sold as souvenirs. Also, a temporary site to store the souvenir items is needed.

Equipment and Supplies: Create appropriate certificates of authenticity and engraved metal plates to be attached to the objects. Posters or flyers may be needed to advertise the fundraiser. If a mail campaign is done, access to a typewriter or computer and an adequate supply of stamps and stationery will also be needed.

Publicity and Promotion: A major campaign should be mounted involving person-to-person sales, sales to businesses, and free publicity in the area news media. A mail campaign to boosters and individuals who have attended athletic events could also be used. Finally, sale of the souvenirs can take place during sporting events themselves. The sales campaign should highlight the suitability and desirability of the souvenir for display in addition to the benefits accruing to the sport or recreation program.

Time: You must deal with three different time frames in this fundraiser. First is the time frame of the demolition itself, the period during which the structure or facility will be torn down or dismantled. The collection of the physical objects must be accomplished during this very specific time period. The second time frame includes the time necessary to refurbish the souvenirs and to have the metal plates and the certificates prepared. This could take up to 3 or 4 weeks depending upon the number of items salvaged. The third time frame revolves around the sales window. The publicized selling window should not exceed 4 to 6 weeks, although the items can continue to be sold until the supply is exhausted.

Expenditures: Minimal expenditures are required. The actual souvenir should cost less than $1 to create, including the completed certificate and the metal plate. The salvaged items should be obtained as donations. Some additional costs may be incurred in terms of posters and flyers and other advertising. Seed money of $250 is sufficient to get this fundraiser off and running. If 2,000 souvenirs are created, the total cost should be in the neighborhood of $3,000 (this figure allows for additional expenses involved in promotional activities, a mail campaign, and so forth).

Personnel (Staff/Volunteers):   About 40 to 60 volunteers supported by 2 to 4 staff members can sell the souvenirs. Supporters who are business owners in the community can display and sell the souvenirs. And, of course, volunteers are needed to collect the objects from the demolition site, store them, and clean and prepare the souvenirs.

Risk Management

There is always a physical risk involved in retrieving objects from any demolition site. Care should be taken to minimize the physical dangers and therefore the legal liability exposure involved in obtaining and in refurbishing the souvenirs. Only adults should retrieve potential souvenirs from the demolition site, and they should do so only after the site has been determined to be safe. Additionally, only adults should be involved in the actual preparation of the souvenirs. Although there is some financial risk involved in this fundraiser, advance sales will help reduce this risk.

Permits/Licenses

Permission to salvage the items should be obtained from the site owner well in advance of the demolition.

Hints

It is helpful to attach a piece of felt to the bottom of the object; this upgrades the appearance and usefulness of the souvenir, which can be proudly displayed in a home or an office. Similarly, a multicolored, professionally created and printed certificate of authenticity is a nice touch. You may have few, if any, actual costs if sufficient, skilled volunteers will donate their competencies.

Ongoing Bingo Contests

68

Potential Net Income

$30,000 annually

Complexity/Degree of Difficulty

High

Description

Weekly, biweekly, or monthly bingo contests are held at the site of the sponsoring athletic or recreation organization. Bingo is a game of chance in which players pay money to place plastic disks on cards that have patterns of numbered squares. The winning player is the first individual in the room to fill in a specific pattern (up, down, across, or diagonal) of numbered squares following the numbers announced by the "caller." You may choose to entice patrons by giving away door prizes as well. Profits, which can be really significant, are realized from the money the participants pay to play each card minus the payout to those who win individual games. If an average of 250 people take part in the bingo games each month the potential profit approaches some $30,000 annually even with a payout of $4,000 in winnings each month. A concession area selling items that are popular in the community will also reap big profits over the long run.

Scheduling

These bingo games can be held on the same Saturday or Sunday afternoon each week or month.

Resources

Facilities: A sufficiently large, open, indoor area is required. Adequate lighting and seating sufficient to handle large crowds must be secured. It is not unusual to have 200 to 300 or more participants taking part.

Equipment and Supplies: The bingo equipment and supplies can be purchased from a variety of sources; check the yellow pages in any large city. Also, a high-quality loudspeaker system pays for itself in the long run. Comfortable chairs and tables or benches will go a long way toward encouraging people to stay for the duration of the afternoon. If items are to be given away as door prizes it will be necessary to secure these prizes at reduced cost or as donations from area businesses.

Publicity and Promotion: After the initial extensive community-wide publicity campaign (via print and air media), these ongoing bingo contests can easily be sustained and can even grow via word-of-mouth advertising supplemented by periodic promotion and publicity. Planning for special promotional giveaways (of donated items) during the games only heightens the anticipation, the excitement, and the enjoyment of those in attendance.

Time: Typically, the afternoon bingo sessions last around 3 to 5 hours. Planning for this type of event can be completed within 1 to 2 weeks. However, the advance publicity surrounding the initial kickoff bingo session might take up considerably more time, such as 3 to 4 weeks, to ensure maximum impact upon the public. Setting up this event and cleaning up afterwards will each take about an hour.

Expenditures: Other than the equipment and periodic advertisements, which will total about $300, there are no other significant initial costs. Prize money is provided from the income generated from the bingo games themselves.

Personnel (Staff/Volunteers):   All staffing of the event can be done by 1 or 2 staff members and 10 to 15 volunteers.

Risk Management

There are actually two major risks facing the sponsoring group. The first risk centers around the competition posed by other bingo games already in operation, especially those sponsored by churches. Find out about potential competitors to see if such competition, if it does exist, might deter you from starting a bingo operation. The second risk involves how the general public will react to a nonprofit sport or recreation group sponsoring a game of chance. You can ascertain this by seeking input from a wide range of constituents and boosters. There is minimal financial risk in this type of fundraiser; similarly, the likelihood of legal liability exposure is low. Be sure that the insurance policy for the site where the bingo games are to be held covers this activity.

Permits/Licenses

For a game of chance, there are invariably permissions to be obtained, legal requirements to meet, and permits or licenses to purchase. Those municipalities and states regulating bingo games frequently also require operators of such games to pay a fee. Normally, these fees are quite reasonable in light of the potential profit accruing to the organization.

Hints

This type of entertainment is more popular in some areas of the country than others. In locations where there are limited recreational opportunities or where the game of bingo is especially popular, the potential for significant profits is very real. The ongoing bingo contests can be a major fundraising effort by the recreation or sport group. Making people aware of the programs that the bingo profits will make possible only increases the acceptance of the total bingo operation. This is because people will be able to have an enjoyable time while knowing that the proceeds will be put to good use within the community.

Dance Marathon

69

Potential Net Income
$35,500

Complexity/Degree of Difficulty
High

Description
Students, coaches, and administrators participate in a dance marathon for which pledges are solicited from area businesses, corporations, and individuals. Pledges are based upon the total number of hours that participants dance (with a 10-minute break provided each hour). Pledges normally range from 10¢ to $1 per hour, although some contributors may pledge more. Thus, an individual who solicits a $5 per hour pledge from a business will generate $120 from that one company alone if the dancer dances for 24 hours (with a 10-minute rest break each hour). Dancers need not dance consecutive hours; an individual might dance for 5 hours and then rest for an hour and continue with an additional 15 hours, for a total of 20 hours. If 300 dancers participate in the marathon and each averages total pledges of just $5 per hour, and if the average number of hours danced totals 24, the total earned is $36,000, for a net income of $35,500.

Scheduling
The dance runs from 6 p.m. on a Friday until 1 a.m. on Sunday, for a total of 31 hours maximum.

Resources
Facilities: The marathon requires a gymnasium or other large facility.

Equipment and Supplies: Suitable lighting and a powerful sound system are a must, as are tables and chairs for participants and spectators. Food and drink (obtained as donations, if possible) must be provided to the dancers throughout the marathon. The music can be provided either by a live band (donated or paid for) or by a disk jockey; the music chosen should be in line with current trends. Appropriate decorations help set the festive mood of this event. Posters and flyers should be distributed throughout the community.

Publicity and Promotion: Because the marathon is being held for a nonprofit group, the local media should provide coverage as a news item or community interest item. This is also a great photo opportunity for area newspapers. Securing a local radio station to cover the marathon by broadcasting during the beginning and the closing hours is a must, because the radio DJs can promote the event prior to as well as during the marathon.

Time: Planning for the event can be completed in as few as 1 to 3 days. Soliciting pledges and making all necessary arrangements will consume 2 to 3 weeks. Setting up for the marathon and cleaning up afterward will each take 2 to 3 hours. The marathon itself consumes 31 hours, which is sufficient to generate big-time profits but not so lengthy as to discourage participants or to dampen the enthusiasm of those taking part.

Expenditures: Expenditures will involve advertising and promotion, unless suitable donations are secured. Food and drink, if not donated, will have to be purchased. Posters and flyers need to be created and distributed within the community. Plan on spending $500 to get the marathon up and running.

Personnel (Staff/Volunteers):   Naturally, the success of this fundraising effort hinges on the effectiveness of the volunteers (students and adults alike) in soliciting pledges. Solicitors of pledges need not participate in the marathon but can seek pledges for other individuals who will participate. A popular master of ceremonies (or perhaps two or three such people) should keep the marathon interesting and lively. Chaperones (1 adult to every 10 youngsters) are also necessary to ensure a safe and enjoyable fundraiser. About 30 volunteers total are necessary when there are 300 dancers.

Risk Management

You need to remain cognizant of health and safety factors involved in this type of marathon. A nurse or other medical worker should be available as a chaperone and to provide assistance if needed. Additionally, plenty of foods and fluids should be made available to the dancers throughout the marathon. The financial risk is minimal due to the fact that initial expenses are not large and the pledges are made prior to the event.

Permits/Licenses

Check with the health department or town clerk to see whether this type of fundraiser requires a special permit or food license.

Hints

The participants in the dance marathon can include adults (coaches and administrators) as well as students. Preparing professional pledge sheets to be used by those soliciting donations will help in terms of record keeping and will upgrade the sophistication and effectiveness of the solicitation process. Remember that not all pledges will actually be collected; there is a high likelihood of some 10% to 15% attrition between the pledges made and the money received. It is helpful to provide informal instruction to those who seek pledges so as to increase their effectiveness and efficiency and to ensure that only appropriate and acceptable tactics are used. A rule that helps control the security and safety dimensions of the dance marathon is that once the participants enter the facility they may not leave and reenter. This cuts down on the possibility of individuals leaving and drinking alcohol and then returning to the dance. Notify the local police to make them aware of the all-night marathon so that extra patrols might be scheduled.

Life Insurance Policy Naming Your Organization as the Beneficiary

70

Potential Net Income

$50,000

Complexity/Degree of Difficulty

High

Description

This fundraising tactic involves convincing a fan, booster, or supporter of the recreation or sport organization to purchase a life insurance policy, naming the organization as the beneficiary. Thus, for a relatively small dollar amount in terms of premiums, the insured can leave $10,000 to $1,000,000 to the organization *and can be recognized for such a sizable donation.*

Scheduling

A volunteer who is influential in the community should meet with potential donors and explain this unique fundraising concept. A lunch or breakfast with two or three potential contributors can create an atmosphere conducive to talking about this subject. The meeting should also be attended by a high-level administrator of the sport or recreation organization.

Resources

Facilities: No specific facilities are needed. The meeting can take place at any site.

Equipment and Supplies: Examples of insurance policies should be used as well as written documentation about how this fundraising device has worked for other nonprofit entities.

Publicity and Promotion: Discrete mention of this type of arrangement can be made at various organizational meetings. If the organization has a newsletter, include in it information about this fundraising technique and how it has helped similar organizations. This can familiarize people with the general concept of the fundraiser.

Time: The cultivation of potential donors is ongoing; don't expect overnight results. It can take weeks, months, and even years of work on this project before an individual elects to participate.

Expenditures: Expenditures center around cultivation activities such as meals and travel. Budget $200 for meals and other incidentals.

Personnel (Staff/Volunteers):   Assisting 2 to 5 professional staff members in soliciting donors should be 3 to 5 influential volunteers who are able to gain access to potential donors. Of course, 1 or 2 insurance experts should be available to provide information and to answer any questions about the life insurance policy as a contribution concept.

Risk Management

Be sure you and your staff and volunteers do not give the impression that you are selling insurance. You merely explain the concept; the donor purchases the insurance policy from a licensed agent. There are no legal risks and minimal financial exposure in this fundraising effort.

Permits/Licenses

None are needed.

Hints

The prospective donors should never be asked to change their existing wills or the beneficiaries of existing life insurance policies. Rather, this fundraising effort centers around the purchase of additional insurance, the proceeds of which are earmarked for the recreation or sport organization.

About the Author

William F. Stier, Jr., EdD, directs the sport management/athletic administration programs at the State University of New York (SUNY), Brockport, where he also serves as the coordinator of sport coaching and as a full professor. While at SUNY, he has also filled the roles of director of intercollegiate athletics, chair of the physical education and sport department, and president of the faculty senate.

Dr. Stier has delivered seminars on fundraising and promotions for the NCAA and the United States Sports Academy. He has also delivered many speeches on fundraising for physical education and sport organizations at the national and international levels. He was one of five sports scholars invited by the United States Olympic Committee to attend the International Olympic Academy in 1990. He is a member of the American Alliance for Health, Physical Education, Recreation and Dance and the National Association for Girls and Women in Sport.

Dr. Stier is a frequent contributor to the professional literature and serves on the editorial boards for *Athletic Management, The Physical Educator, Annual of Applied Research in Coaching and Athletics,* and *Sport Marketing Quarterly*. He is listed in the *Marquis Who's Who in American Education*.